CREATE AND UPDATE

AN UNRESOURCED PROJECT

USING

ELECOSOFT (ASTA) POWERPROJECT

VERSION 17

BY

PAUL EASTWOOD HARRIS

2-day training course

handout and student workshops

ASTA NAME CHANGE

Asta plc was purchased by Elecosoft plc and the term Asta has been dropped in all text published by Elecosoft plc in Powerproject Version 15. Many people and most overseas authorised distributor websites at the time of publishing this book refer to Powerproject as "Asta" so as a result I have named this book with the term "Asta".

DISCLAIMER

The information contained in this book is, to the best of the author's knowledge, true and correct. The author has made every effort to ensure accuracy of this publication but cannot be held responsible for any loss or damage arising from any information in this book.

AUTHOR AND PUBLISHER

Paul E Harris
Eastwood Harris Pty Ltd
PO Box 4032
Doncaster Heights 3109
Victoria
Australia
harrispe@eh.com.au
http://www.eh.com.au
Tel: +61 (0)4 1118 7701

12 January 2024

ISBN 978-0-6486355-2-9 (0-6486355-2-X)

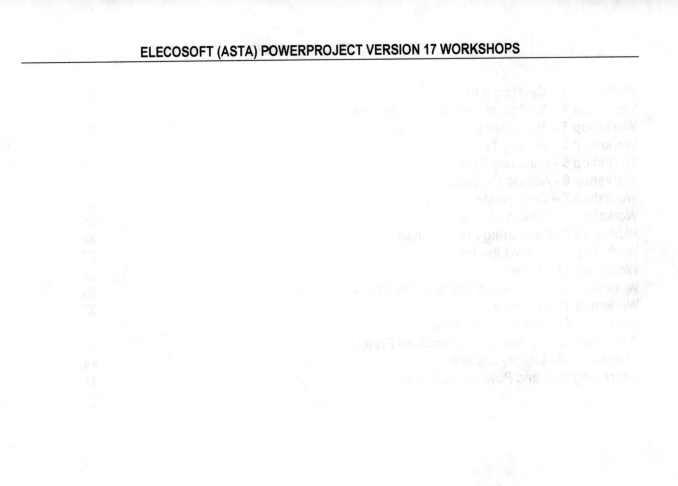

Workshop 1 – Creating a Project

Notes on Date Format
The date format displayed in Asta dialogue boxes, such as the **Start Date** in the **File, New** form, is adopted from your **System Short Date** format. You may change your **System Short Date** from **Start, Settings, Time and Language** in earlier Windows operating systems and in later Windows operating systems in **Settings, Region, Change date, time or number formats**. This change will also change the date format in many apps such as **File Explorer** and **Outlook**.

The workshops text displays the format of dd-MMM-yy and display dates as 09-Dec-24.

Note: There are some slides with the date format of dd-mm-yy, 09-12-24.

Background
You are an employee of OzBuild Ltd and are responsible for planning the bid preparation required to ensure that a response to an RFQ (Request For Quote) for Wilson International is submitted on time.

Your company has completed the Start-up Phase of the project, the Bid Strategy has been developed and approval to bid for this project has been given.

You have been requested to plan the project Bid Phase, where the Bid will be produced, which comprises of the following deliverables/products:
- Technical Specification
- Delivery Plan
- Bid Document.

You have been advised that the RFQ will not be available until the 06 December 2027.

These workshops will take you through the process of creating the Initiating Phase Plan for the development of the Bid to be submitted in response to the RFQ.

 A project template in *.pp format titled "Australian and US Version 17 Asta Powerproject construction template" has been loaded on the Eastwood Harris web site at www.eh.com.au **Software Downloads** page that has a number of the issues with trying to use the UK templates in the US or Australia resolved, including the default currency has been set to $'s and calendar holidays revised. You should download this file, open it and save it as a template and use this file instead of the Asta supplied UK templates.

If you do not use this template you will receive different results.

If you use a different currency then you may create your countries currency and assign it and still use this template.

Assignment

1. Download the Powerproject template "Australian and US Powerproject Version 17 construction template" has been loaded on the Eastwood Harris web site at www.eh.com.au Software Downloads page, or use a template supplied by your trainer.

2. Open the template and save in the Powerproject Templates directory or drag this template in the directory set in your **File**, **Options**, **File Locations**:

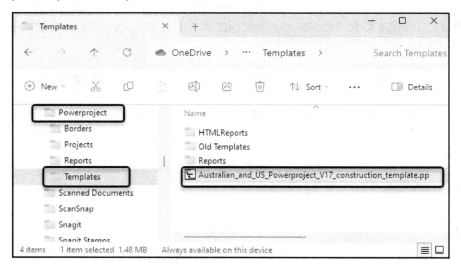

3. Close all projects.
4. Create a new project by selecting **File**, **New** and select an appropriate template,
5. Create your project with the file name of **OzBuild** in a location of your choice, such as the desktop,
6. Title – **OzBuild Bid**,
7. For – **Wilson International**,
8. By – enter your name,
9. Set the **Start date:** to **Mon 06 Dec 27,**
10. Press the **Create** button to save the data.

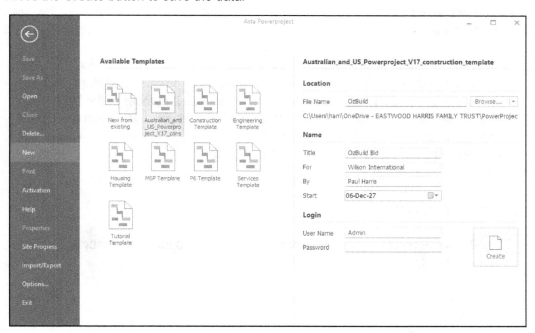

---

11. Check the currency unit of Dollar exists by selecting **View**, **Show**, **Library Explorer**:

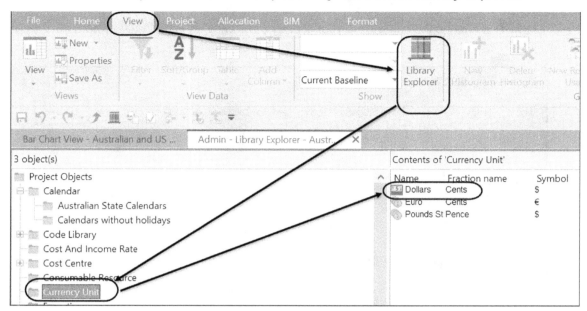

12. An additional window and tab is now open, you may close this by clicking on the **X**:

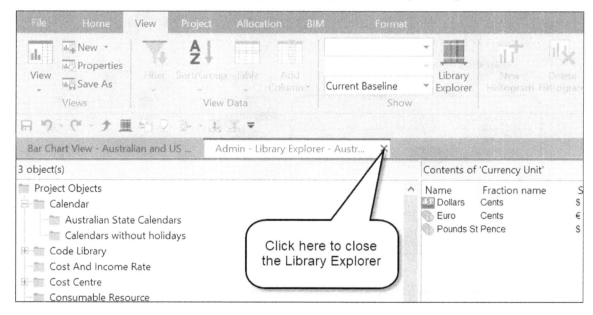

13. Add your countries currency if it does not exist.

14. Select **File**, **Options**, **View** tab and check that your countries currency is set as the **Default Currency**.

15. If you wish to change the currency to your country's currency, then do that now from the drop down box.

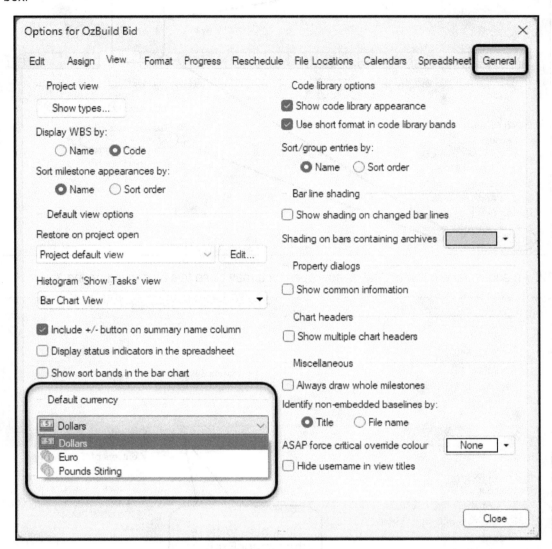

NOTE: Completed workshops and PowerPoint Instructors slide presentations may be downloaded from the Eastwood Harris web site at www.eh.com.au.

Workshop 2 – Navigation and Setting Options

Background
In this workshop you will also practice navigating around the screen.

Navigation Practice
1. Click on the Ribbon Toolbar menu at the top of the screen, click on all the tabs and observe which commands are located on each tab:

2. When you load Add-Ins loaded or a BIM license you will see an extra **Add-Ins** or **BIM** tab:

3. Right-click on the Ribbon Toolbar and display the Ribbon Toolbar Menu:

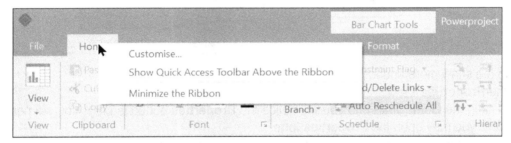

4. To allow more buttons to be displayed on the **Quick Access Toolbar**, click on the **Show Quick Access Toolbar Below the Ribbon** to move the **Quick Access Toolbar** below the **Ribbon Toolbar**.
5. Click on the **Customise...** to open the **Ribbon Customisation** form. Explore the tabs on the left-hand side.
6. The Eastwood Harris Asta Powerproject Version 17 Quick Access Toolbar has been created to make using Powerproject simpler. Download this file from www.eh.com.au **Software and Downloads** page, unzip it by double clicking on it and dragging the XML file to your desktop.
7. Then import the toolbar into Asta by right clicking on your Asta Quick Access toolbar to open the **Ribbon Customisation** form and selecting **Customise...**, **Ribbon**, **Import/Export**.
8. Right-click on the Ribbon Toolbar and display the Ribbon Toolbar Menu. Click on **Minimise the Ribbon** to hide the Ribbon Toolbar.
9. Click in a column header to display a double headed arrow ↔ and move the column to a different position by dragging.
10. Resize the **Date Zone** (timescale) by clicking on a tick mark in the **Date Zone** to display a double headed arrow and dragging left and right.
11. Move the left and right by left clicking in the timescale and when the Hand 🖐 icon is displayed drag the timescale left and right.

12. Right Click in the Gantt Chart and select **Properties View** to split the screen:

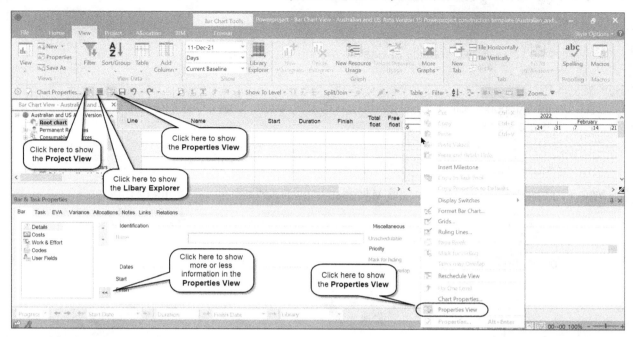

13. Click on the show more and less information button.
14. Close the **Properties View**.
15. Right Click in the Gantt Chart and you will notice the **Properties** button is grey. You will need to add a task before you may open the **Properties** form.
16. Click on the **Projects View** button to hide and display the **Projects View,** this is where you access the calendars, resources and codes etc.

Workshop 3 – Maintaining the Calendars

Background

The normal working week at OzBuild Ltd is Monday to Friday, 8 hours per day excluding Public Holidays. The installation staff work Monday to Saturday, 8 hours per day.

Assignment

The company observes the following holidays:

	2024	2025	2026	2027	2028
New Year's Day	1 January	1 January	1 January	1 January	3 January*
Easter	29 March- 1 April	18 - 21 April	3 - 6 April	26 - 29 March	14-17 April
Christmas Day	25 December	25 December	25 December	27 December*	25 December
Boxing Day	26 December	26 December	28 December*	28 December*	26 December

* These holidays occur on a weekend and the dates in the table above have been moved to the next weekday.

NOTE: Boxing Day, the day after Christmas, is a holiday celebrated in many countries.

Assignment

1. Open the **Library Explorer**.
2. Copy and paste an existing 5-day week, 8 hour per day calendar that does not have holidays into the Calendar root directory. You could use the **5 Day Week No Hols** calendar.
3. Rename to create a calendar titled **OzBuild 5 day/week** which has an 8 hour per day.
4. Open the calendar **Properties** form,
5. Assign the holidays for 2027 and 2028 by Clt clicking on all the holidays in each year,

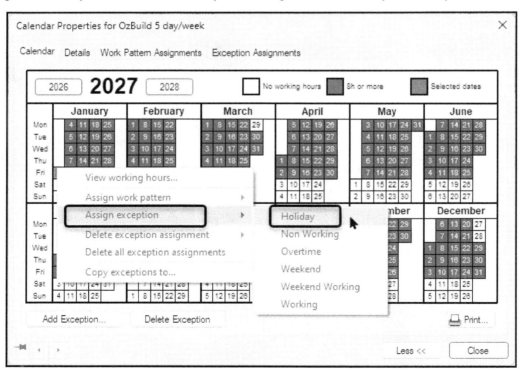

---

6.   Then select **Assign exception**, **Holiday**,
7.   Then right click **From work pattern periods** for morning and afternoon and click on **Add**:

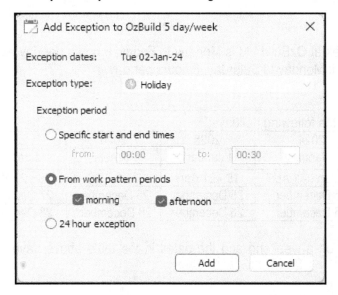

8.   Delete any holidays not required.
9.   Copy and paste the **OzBuild 5 day/week** to create a calendar and name **OzBuild 6 day/week**.
10. Assign the **8hr-day, 6day Week Work Pattern** from the **Calendar Properties**, **Work Pattern Assignments tab.**
11. Add the Easter Saturday Holidays for both 2027 and 2028.
12. Ensure 1 January 2028 is made into a holiday.
13. Close the **Library Explorer**.
14. Make the **OzBuild 5 day/week** calendar the **Task Default** by right clicking on the calendar,
15. Check all the boxes in the **Calendar Settings** form:

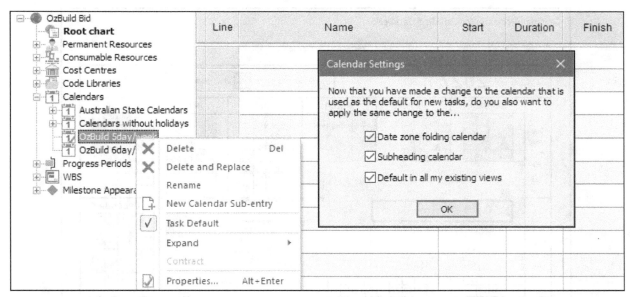

16. Save your project.
17. Check your calendars using the pictures below.

Answers to Workshop 3

OzBuild 5 Day/Week

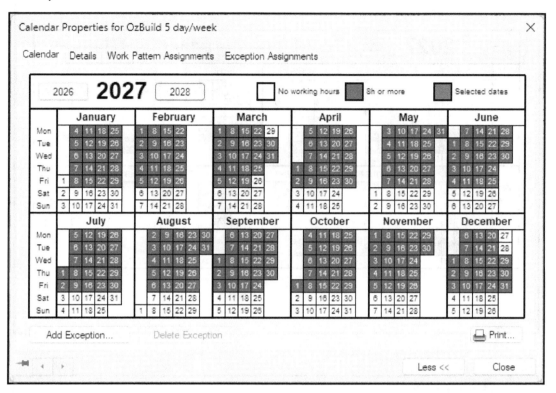

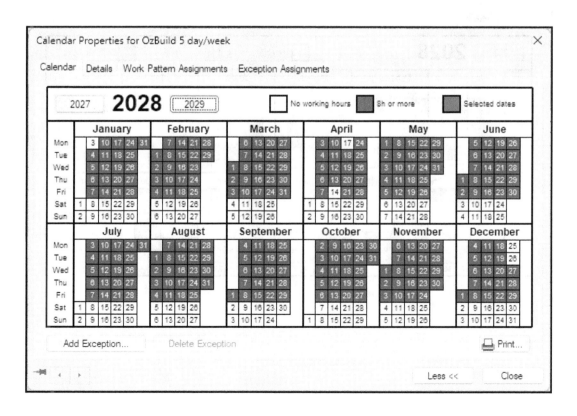

OzBuild 6 Day/Week

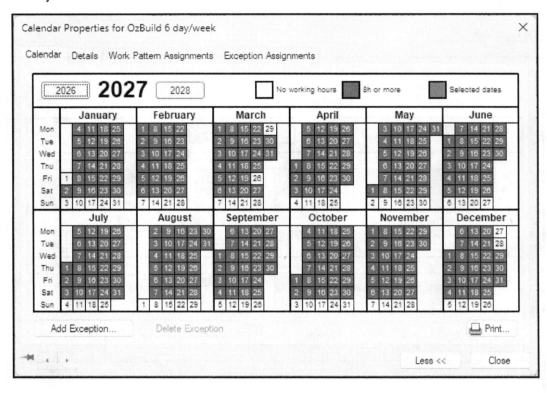

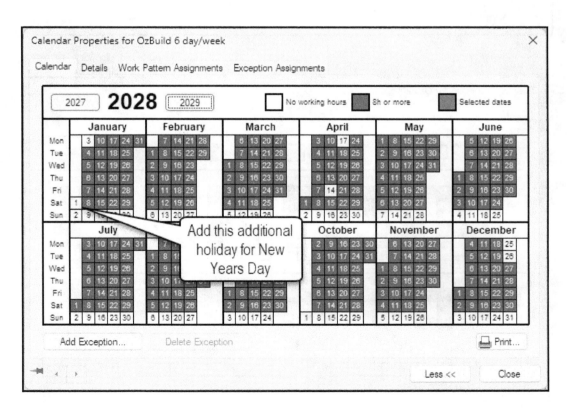

Workshop 4 – Adding Tasks

Background

If you do not use the same template as the one that was used to create the screenshots in this book you may receive a different result.

It is simpler to teach Asta Powerproject by showing how to enter the tasks first and then showing the creation of summary tasks to represent the WBS Nodes or Products or Deliverables second. Once a user understands the process then the tasks and summary tasks may be entered in any order.

Assignment

1. We will assume that the Planning Process is complete and we are to produce a schedule with several tasks for each Product (Deliverable) in the Work Breakdown Structure – WBS.
2. Check the **OzBuild 5 day/week** is set as the **Task Default**, it should have a red tick on the right of the name:

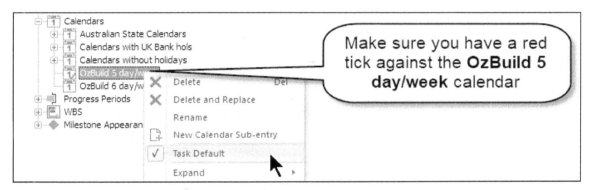

3. If it is not, then set it as the **Task Default.**
4. Check all the boxes in the **Calendar Settings** form:

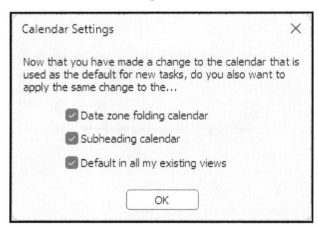

5. Use the columns to enter the **Name** and **Duration** of the tasks as below.
6. A task will become a milestone when assigned a zero duration.

ID	Task Name	Duration	Task Calendar
1	Approval to Bid	0 days	
2	Determine Installation Requirements	4 days	
3	Create Technical Specification	5 days	
4	Identify Supplier Components	2 days	
5	Validate Technical Specification	2 days	
6	Document Delivery Methodology	4 days	
7	Obtain Quotes from Suppliers	8 days	
8	Calculate the Bid Estimate	3 days	Assign the 6 Days Working Week calendar
9	Create the Project Schedule	3 days	Assign the 6 Days Working Week calendar
10	Review the Delivery Plan	1 day	
11	Create Draft of Bid Document	6 days	
12	Review Bid Document	4 days	
13	Finalize and Submit Bid Document	2 days	
14	Bid Document Submitted	0 days	Make into a Finish Milestone

7. The estimate and schedule tasks will be completed by site personnel who work a 6-day week.

8. Select the **Calculate the Bid Estimate** and **Create the Project Schedule** task bars or Line Numbers.

9. Assign the OzBuild 6 day/week calendar, drag this calendar onto the selected bars and select the option of **Retain the existing duration and change the dates if necessary**.

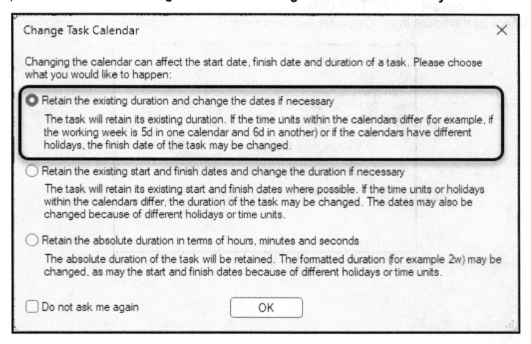

10. Select **No,** not change the **Folding Calendar**.

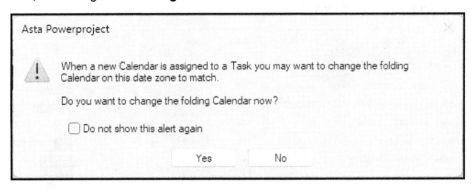

11. Make the Bid Document Submitted into a **Finish Milestone** by right clicking on the Milestone icon:

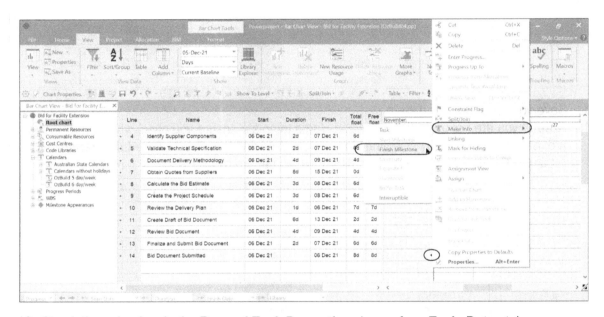

12. Check the calendars in the **Bar and Task Properties** view or form **Task**, **Dates** tab:

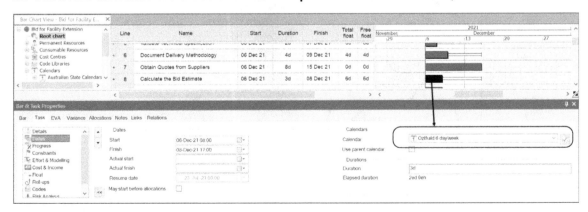

13. Press **F9** to schedule, if a popup box asks to run a **Reschedule Report** then select **OFF** to cancel it and your schedule should look like this:

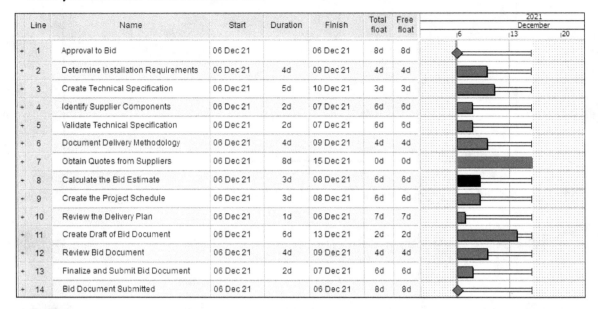

Line	Name	Start	Duration	Finish	Total float	Free float
1	Approval to Bid	06 Dec 21		06 Dec 21	8d	8d
2	Determine Installation Requirements	06 Dec 21	4d	09 Dec 21	4d	4d
3	Create Technical Specification	06 Dec 21	5d	10 Dec 21	3d	3d
4	Identify Supplier Components	06 Dec 21	2d	07 Dec 21	6d	6d
5	Validate Technical Specification	06 Dec 21	2d	07 Dec 21	6d	6d
6	Document Delivery Methodology	06 Dec 21	4d	09 Dec 21	4d	4d
7	Obtain Quotes from Suppliers	06 Dec 21	8d	15 Dec 21	0d	0d
8	Calculate the Bid Estimate	06 Dec 21	3d	08 Dec 21	6d	6d
9	Create the Project Schedule	06 Dec 21	3d	08 Dec 21	6d	6d
10	Review the Delivery Plan	06 Dec 21	1d	06 Dec 21	7d	7d
11	Create Draft of Bid Document	06 Dec 21	6d	13 Dec 21	2d	2d
12	Review Bid Document	06 Dec 21	4d	09 Dec 21	4d	4d
13	Finalize and Submit Bid Document	06 Dec 21	2d	07 Dec 21	6d	6d
14	Bid Document Submitted	06 Dec 21		06 Dec 21	8d	8d

14. Save your **OzBuild Bid** project.
15. **Note:** If you are not using the Eastwood Harris template ensure you check you scheduling options are the same as below by selecting **Home**, **Schedule** and from the **Reschedule Branch** drop down list select **Options…**, and ensure that they are as per the picture below:

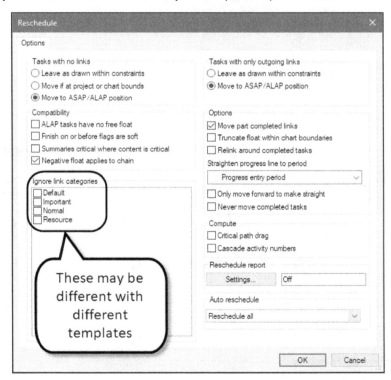

Workshop 5 - Summary Tasks

Background
The summary tasks may be used to represent a Project, Deliverables/Products, WBS Nodes, Phase, Stages or Work Packages.

We will add summary tasks to represent the Initiation Phase and Deliverables/Products of the Initiation Phase.

Assignment

1. Create a Summary Level 1 for Phase entitled **Bid for Facility Extension** and
2. Create a Summary Level 2 for each of the three Products:
   - **Technical Specification**
   - **Delivery Plan**
   - **Bid Document**
3. Try using the various methods for indenting and outdenting tasks.
4. Your schedule should look like this:

Line	Name	Start	Duration	Finish	Total float	Free float
1	⊟ Bid for Facility Extension	06 Dec 27	8d	15 Dec 27	0d	0d
2	⊟ Technical Specification	06 Dec 27	5d	10 Dec 27	3d	3d
3	Approval to Bid	06 Dec 27		06 Dec 27	8d	8d
4	Determine Installation Requirement	06 Dec 27	4d	09 Dec 27	4d	4d
5	Create Technical Specification	06 Dec 27	5d	10 Dec 27	3d	3d
6	Identify Supplier Components	06 Dec 27	2d	07 Dec 27	6d	6d
7	Validate Technical Specification	06 Dec 27	2d	07 Dec 27	6d	6d
8	⊟ Delivery Plan	06 Dec 27	8d	15 Dec 27	0d	0d
9	Document Delivery Methodology	06 Dec 27	4d	09 Dec 27	4d	4d
10	Obtain Quotes from Suppliers	06 Dec 27	8d	15 Dec 27	0d	0d
11	Calculate the Bid Estimate	06 Dec 27	3d	08 Dec 27	6d	6d
12	Create the Project Schedule	06 Dec 27	3d	08 Dec 27	6d	6d
13	Review the Delivery Plan	06 Dec 27	1d	06 Dec 27	7d	7d
14	⊟ Bid Document	06 Dec 27	6d	13 Dec 27	2d	2d
15	Create Draft of Bid Document	06 Dec 27	6d	13 Dec 27	2d	2d
16	Review Bid Document	06 Dec 27	4d	09 Dec 27	4d	4d
17	Finalize and Submit Bid Document	06 Dec 27	2d	07 Dec 27	6d	6d
18	Bid Document Submitted	06 Dec 27		06 Dec 27	8d	8d

5. Use the **Show to** level button to summerise the schedule:

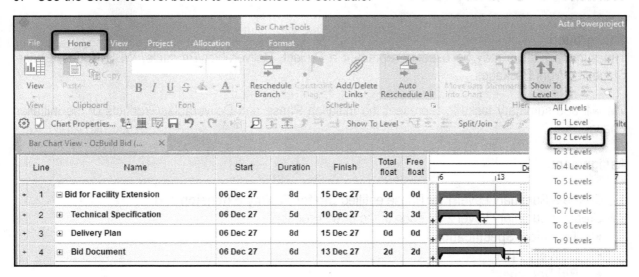

6. Save your **OzBuild Bid** project.
7. **Note:** The Root Chart may be renamed to produce a Level 1 WBS Node.

Workshop 6 - Adding the Links

Background
You have determined the logical sequence of tasks, so you may now enter the links.

Assignment
1. Ensure you have the last workshop file open.
2. Select the **Root Chart** node in the **Project View** so the Line Numbers match the picture below.
3. Input the logic below using several of the methods detailed in this chapter.
4. Use the Zoom Slider at the bottom left hand side of the screen to make the bars larger which in turn makes assigning links graphically easier:

Line	Name	Predecessors	Predecessors
1	⊟ Bid for Facility Extension		
2	⊟ Technical Specification		
3	Approval to Bid		
4	Determine Installation Requirements	3	Approval to Bid
5	Create Technical Specification	4	Determine Installation Requirements
6	Identify Supplier Components	5	Create Technical Specification
7	Validate Technical Specification	6	Identify Supplier Components
8	⊟ Delivery Plan		
9	Document Delivery Methodology	7	Validate Technical Specification
10	Obtain Quotes from Suppliers	6	Identify Supplier Components
11	Calculate the Bid Estimate	9, 10	Document Delivery Methodology, Obtain Quotes from Suppliers
12	Create the Project Schedule	11	Calculate the Bid Estimate
13	Review the Delivery Plan	12	Create the Project Schedule
14	⊟ Bid Document		
15	Create Draft of Bid Document	9	Document Delivery Methodology
16	Review Bid Document	13, 15	Review the Delivery Plan, Create Draft of Bid Document
17	Finalize and Submit Bid Document	16	Review Bid Document
18	Bid Document Submitted	17	Finalize and Submit Bid Document

5. You may wish to apply a **View** with an appropriate table or a **Table** to add and review your logic. If you have used the Eastwood Harris template, then you may apply **Logic – Pres & Succ (Line No) Table:**

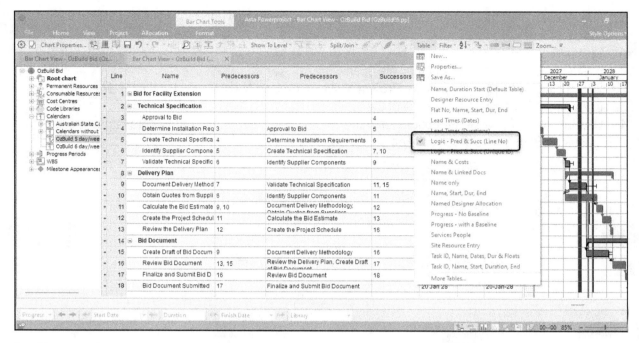

6. If you apply another **View** then you will end up with multiple tabs open and you may close any you do not need:

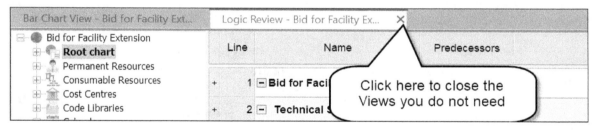

7. Press **F9** to calculate the schedule, and accept the defaults:

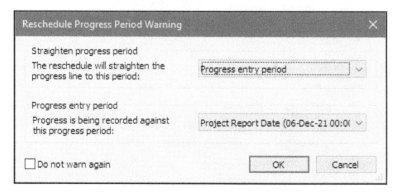

8. Accept the defaults and click OK.
9. If you receive a schedule report warning, you may wish to click on **Off** so you are not presented with the report in the future.

10. You should reapply the original **Table** or **View** and check your dates. The **Bar Chart** View and the **Task ID, Name, Dates, Dur & Float** Table give the result below:

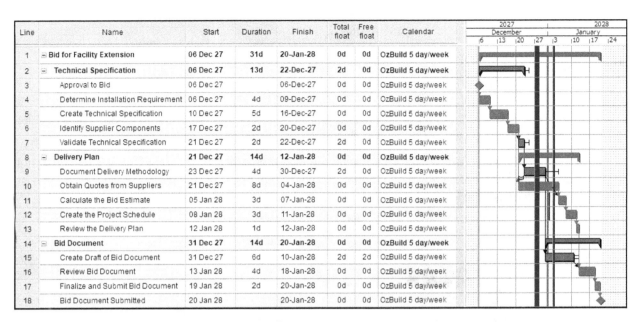

Line	Name	Start	Duration	Finish	Total float	Free float	Calendar
1	⊟ Bid for Facility Extension	06 Dec 27	31d	20-Jan-28	0d	0d	OzBuild 5 day/week
2	⊟ Technical Specification	06 Dec 27	13d	22-Dec-27	2d	0d	OzBuild 5 day/week
3	Approval to Bid	06 Dec 27		06-Dec-27	0d	0d	OzBuild 5 day/week
4	Determine Installation Requirement	06 Dec 27	4d	09-Dec-27	0d	0d	OzBuild 5 day/week
5	Create Technical Specification	10 Dec 27	5d	16-Dec-27	0d	0d	OzBuild 5 day/week
6	Identify Supplier Components	17 Dec 27	2d	20-Dec-27	0d	0d	OzBuild 5 day/week
7	Validate Technical Specification	21 Dec 27	2d	22-Dec-27	2d	0d	OzBuild 5 day/week
8	⊟ Delivery Plan	21 Dec 27	14d	12-Jan-28	0d	0d	OzBuild 5 day/week
9	Document Delivery Methodology	23 Dec 27	4d	30-Dec-27	2d	0d	OzBuild 5 day/week
10	Obtain Quotes from Suppliers	21 Dec 27	8d	04-Jan-28	0d	0d	OzBuild 5 day/week
11	Calculate the Bid Estimate	05 Jan 28	3d	07-Jan-28	0d	0d	OzBuild 6 day/week
12	Create the Project Schedule	08 Jan 28	3d	11-Jan-28	0d	0d	OzBuild 6 day/week
13	Review the Delivery Plan	12 Jan 28	1d	12-Jan-28	0d	0d	OzBuild 5 day/week
14	⊟ Bid Document	31 Dec 27	14d	20-Jan-28	0d	0d	OzBuild 5 day/week
15	Create Draft of Bid Document	31 Dec 27	6d	10-Jan-28	2d	2d	OzBuild 5 day/week
16	Review Bid Document	13 Jan 28	4d	18-Jan-28	0d	0d	OzBuild 5 day/week
17	Finalize and Submit Bid Document	19 Jan 28	2d	20-Jan-28	0d	0d	OzBuild 5 day/week
18	Bid Document Submitted	20 Jan 28		20-Jan-28	0d	0d	OzBuild 5 day/week

11. If you lose the date formatting this will be because the date formatting is saved with the **View** and not the **Table** or you are using a different template. You may reformat the dates by either:

   a. Re applying the **Bar Chart** View, or

   b. Right clicking on the Start and Finish column headers and open the **Format Cells** form:

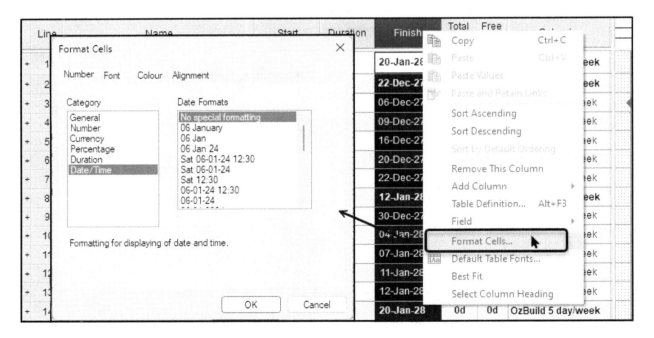

12. Save your OzBuild Bid project.

Workshop 7 – Constraints

Background
Management has provided further input to your schedule and the client requires the submission on or before the 27 Jan 22.

.

Assignment

1. Observe the calculated finish and the Critical Path before applying any constraints.

2. Apply a **Finish on or Before** constraint (also known as a **Finish No Later Than** and a **Late Finish** constraint) with a constraint date of 27 Jan 28 to task **Bid Document Submitted** task.

3. If you are presented with an error message, read the message carefully and then set the constraint. Now review float, there should be no change in the Total Float. This demonstrates that a **Finish on or Before** constraint is after the calculated early finish date does not create positive float.

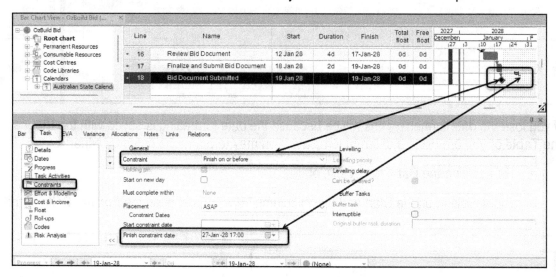

4. Open the **Schedule Options** form and ensure that **Negative float applies to chain** is **NOT** checked:

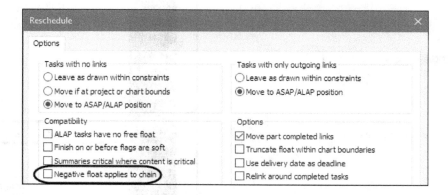

5. Due to proximity to Christmas, management has requested we delay task **Obtain Quotes from Suppliers** until first thing in the New Year, 04 Jan 28. It is hoped that lower prices will be obtained after the Christmas rush.

6. To achieve this, set a **Start on or after** constraint (also known as a **Start No Earlier Than** or **Early Start**) and a constraint date of 04 Jan 28 on task **Obtain Quotes from Suppliers**.

7. You may record this decision in the task notes.

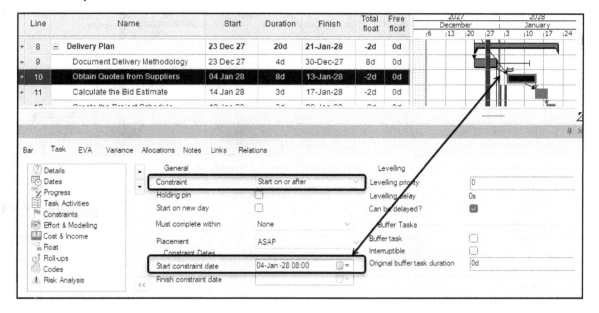

8. Press F9 to reschedule.

9. Should you be presented with an error message,

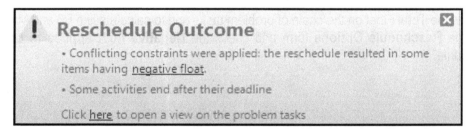

10. Select "**here**" and a new widow will be presented with a new **Reschedule View** one problem activity highlighted:

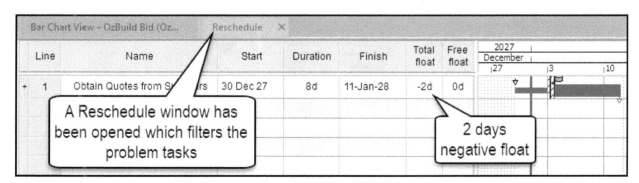

11. When the **Schedule Options** have **Negative float applies to chain** is **NOT** checked, then the software **DOES NOT** calculate like P6 and Microsoft Project and will only display the first problem task with negative float and a negative float bar.

12. Close the **Reschedule** tab and observe the impact on the Critical Path and end dates.

Line	Name	Start	Duration	Finish	Total float	Free float
1	⊟ Bid for Facility Extension	06 Dec 27	36d	27-Jan-28	0d	0d
2	⊟ Technical Specification	06 Dec 27	13d	22-Dec-27	7d	0d
3	Approval to Bid	06 Dec 27		06-Dec-27	5d	0d
4	Determine Installation Requirements	06 Dec 27	4d	09-Dec-27	5d	0d
5	Create Technical Specification	10 Dec 27	5d	16-Dec-27	5d	0d
6	Identify Supplier Components	17 Dec 27	2d	20-Dec-27	5d	0d
7	Validate Technical Specification	21 Dec 27	2d	22-Dec-27	7d	0d
8	⊟ Delivery Plan	23 Dec 27	17d	19-Jan-28	0d	0d
9	Document Delivery Methodology	23 Dec 27	4d	30-Dec-27	7d	0d
10	Obtain Quotes from Suppliers	30 Dec 27	8d	11-Jan-28	-2d	0d
11	Calculate the Bid Estimate	12 Jan 28	3d	14-Jan-28	0d	0d
12	Create the Project Schedule	15 Jan 28	3d	18-Jan-28	0d	0d
13	Review the Delivery Plan	19 Jan 28	1d	19-Jan-28	0d	0d
14	⊟ Bid Document	31 Dec 27	19d	27-Jan-28	0d	0d
15	Create Draft of Bid Document	31 Dec 27	6d	10-Jan-28	7d	7d
16	Review Bid Document	20 Jan 28	4d	25-Jan-28	0d	0d
17	Finalize and Submit Bid Document	26 Jan 28	2d	27-Jan-28	0d	0d
18	Bid Document Submitted	27 Jan 28		27-Jan-28	0d	0d

13. There is 2 days negative float on the **Obtain Quotes from Suppliers** which is scheduled to start on 30 Dec 27 the **Bid Document Submitted** is scheduled on the constraint date and this is not how P6 and Microsoft Project schedules. Finish Constraint acts like a hard constraint and tasks are moved forward in time and the Start Constraint is overridden.

14. To show the Total Float on the chain of problem tasks and to calculate like P6 and Microsoft Project open the **Reschedule Options** form and check the **Negative float applies to chain** and then reschedule.

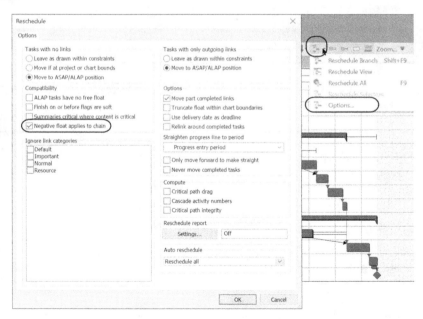

15. Press F9 to Reschedule.

16. The programme will calculate Total Float and dates like Microsoft Project or P6. The Start Constraint is acknowledged, and the Finish Constraint overridden. There is 2 days negative float on the **Obtain Quotes from Suppliers** which is scheduled to start on 4 Jan 28, the constraint date, and the **Bid Document Submitted** is scheduled on 31 Jan 28. The Reschedule tab shows negative float against the chain of problem tasks in the spreadsheet but the Gantt Chart will **NOT** show a Negative Float bar against any of the tasks:

Line	Name	Start	Duration	Finish	Total float	Free float
1	⊟ Bid for Facility Extension	06 Dec 27	38d	31-Jan-28	-2d	0d
2	⊟ Delivery Plan	23 Dec 27	19d	21-Jan-28	-2d	0d
3	Obtain Quotes from Suppliers	04 Jan 28	8d	13-Jan-28	-2d	0d
4	Calculate the Bid Estimate	14 Jan 28	3d	17-Jan-28	-2d	0d
5	Create the Project Schedule	18 Jan 28	3d	20-Jan-28	-2d	0d
6	Review the Delivery Plan	21 Jan 28	1d	21-Jan-28	-2d	0d
7	⊟ Bid Document	31 Dec 27	21d	31-Jan-28	-2d	0d
8	Review Bid Document	24 Jan 28	4d	27-Jan-28	-2d	0d
9	Finalize and Submit Bid Docum	28 Jan 28	2d	31-Jan-28	-2d	0d
10	Bid Document Submitted	31 Jan 28		31-Jan-28	-2d	0d

17. **Note:** The author has raised an enhancement request with Asta to display the Negative Float Bar against all tasks with negative float when **Negative float applies to chain** is checked.

18. After review, it is agreed that 2 days can be deducted from task Review Bid Document. Change the duration of this task to 2 days.

19. Reschedule and you will notice that the Total Float of all critical tasks is now zero and the Critical Path runs between the two tasks with constraints.

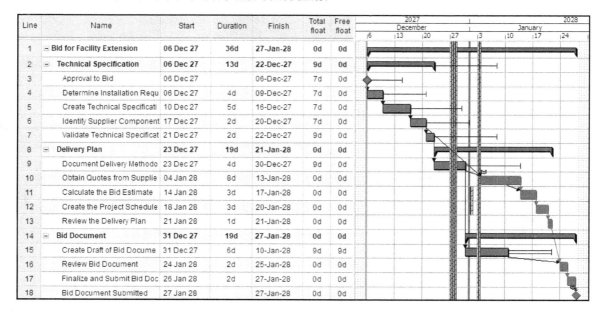

Line	Name	Start	Duration	Finish	Total float	Free float
1	⊟ Bid for Facility Extension	06 Dec 27	36d	27-Jan-28	0d	0d
2	⊟ Technical Specification	06 Dec 27	13d	22-Dec-27	9d	0d
3	Approval to Bid	06 Dec 27		06-Dec-27	7d	0d
4	Determine Installation Requ	06 Dec 27	4d	09-Dec-27	7d	0d
5	Create Technical Specificati	10 Dec 27	5d	16-Dec-27	7d	0d
6	Identify Supplier Component	17 Dec 27	2d	20-Dec-27	7d	0d
7	Validate Technical Specificat	21 Dec 27	2d	22-Dec-27	9d	0d
8	⊟ Delivery Plan	23 Dec 27	19d	21-Jan-28	0d	0d
9	Document Delivery Methodo	23 Dec 27	4d	30-Dec-27	9d	0d
10	Obtain Quotes from Supplie	04 Jan 28	8d	13-Jan-28	0d	0d
11	Calculate the Bid Estimate	14 Jan 28	3d	17-Jan-28	0d	0d
12	Create the Project Schedule	18 Jan 28	3d	20-Jan-28	0d	0d
13	Review the Delivery Plan	21 Jan 28	1d	21-Jan-28	0d	0d
14	⊟ Bid Document	31 Dec 27	19d	27-Jan-28	0d	0d
15	Create Draft of Bid Docume	31 Dec 27	6d	10-Jan-28	9d	9d
16	Review Bid Document	24 Jan 28	2d	25-Jan-28	0d	0d
17	Finalize and Submit Bid Doc	26 Jan 28	2d	27-Jan-28	0d	0d
18	Bid Document Submitted	27 Jan 28		27-Jan-28	0d	0d

20. You may end up with a number of tabs open and it is suggested you close all the ones you do not need.

21. Save your **OzBuild Bid** project.

Workshop 8 - Other task Types

You will go through the process of creating the following in your schedule:

- Task-per-line mode
- Expanded Tasks
- Hammock Tasks
- Task Names as Headers Only

Task-per-line mode

1. Select the second blank line after your last task.
2. Draw 5 tasks on your Gantt chart which have the duration of 5, 2, 1, 7 and 1 day long on one line,
3. Enter a Name of **Concrete Pour**:

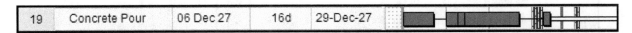

19	Concrete Pour	06 Dec 27	16d	29-Dec-27	

4. Click on the + sign to the left of the Line No and type in the new task names:

19	Form	06 Dec 27	5d	10-Dec-27	
20	Reo	13 Dec 27	2d	14-Dec-27	
21	Pour	15 Dec 27	1d	15-Dec-27	
22	Cure	16 Dec 27	7d	24-Dec-27	
23	Strip	29 Dec 27	1d	29-Dec-27	

5. Assign a 7 day per week calendar to the Cure task, accept the default and DO NOT change the Folding Calendar.

6. You will see the schedule shortens and there are no holidays shown for the Cure task because Powerproject displays the Non Work time against each task:

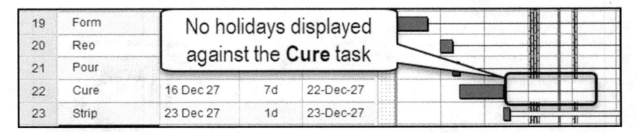

19	Form				
20	Reo				
21	Pour				
22	Cure	16 Dec 27	7d	22-Dec-27	
23	Strip	23 Dec 27	1d	23-Dec-27	

No holidays displayed against the **Cure** task

Note: There are no links and they have an inherited Finish to Start link.

Expanded Tasks

1. Add a new task named **Concrete Pour** in the second blank line below your last task with a duration of 5 days,

2. Right click and select **Make Into** and **Expanded** task:

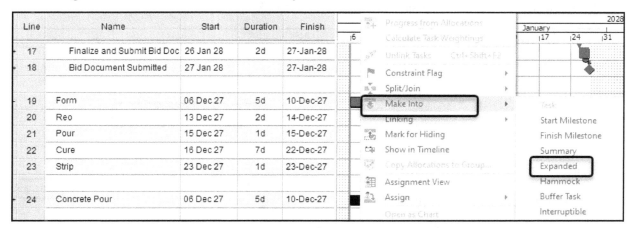

3. Double click on the Concrete Pour task bar to open a new window,

4. Add the same five tasks, link them and assign the 7 day per week to the Cure task, do not change the Folding Calendar.

5. Open the **Project View** and expand the heading **Root Chart**.

6. Click on the all the headings individually from OzBuild to Concrete Pour and you will see how the **Root Chart** works and how **Expanded Task** operate.

7. Select **Root Chart** and **Concrete Pour** in the Project View and see that the Expanded Concrete Pour activities are below the Expanded task.

8. Select **Bid for Facility Extension** and **Concrete Pour** in the Project View and see that the Expanded Concrete Pour activities are at the bottom of the list of tasks:

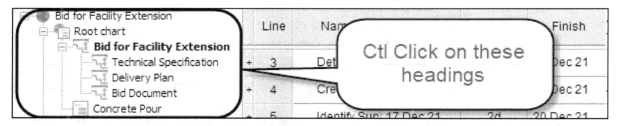

Hammock Tasks

1. Select the **Root Chart** heading,
2. Add a task in the second blank line below your last task named **Supplier Involvement** and assign a duration of 5d,
3. Right click on the bar and select **Make Into**, **Hammock**:

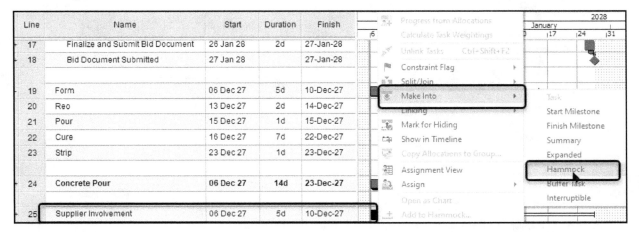

4. Note the change in shape of the Hammock bar,
5. Select the following task bars in the Gantt Chart:
   - Identify Supplier Components
   - Obtain Quotes from Suppliers
   - Create the Project Schedule.
6. Right click and select **Add to Hammock**, select the **Supplier Involvement** task and select OK:

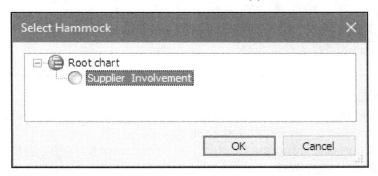

7. Your schedule should look like this:

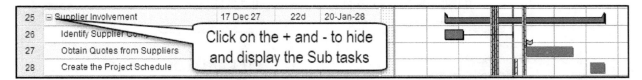

8. The tasks that are part of the Hammock may be seen twice, once in the schedule and once under the Hammock.
9. Click on the sign to the left of the Hammock name to hide or display the Hammock sub tasks:

Task Names as Headers Only

10. When a blank line is created and only a Name is entered and no duration then this becomes a heading only.

11. The picture below shows two headings titled Concrete Pour 1 and Concrete Pour 2, and they have no bar in the Gantt chart:

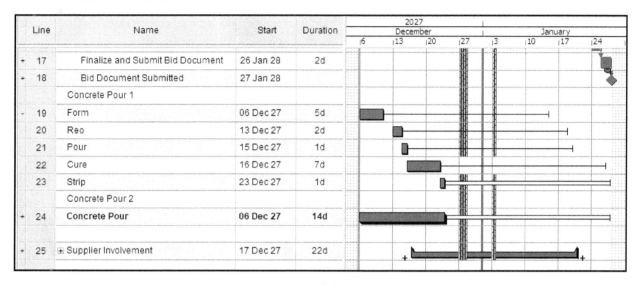

12. Now delete all the tasks you have created in this workshop:

- Task-per-line mode,

- Expanded Tasks,

- Hammock Tasks, ensure you do not select the Hammock sub tasks.

Workshop 9 - Formatting the Bar Chart

Background

Management has received your draft report and requests some changes to the presentation.

Assignment

Format your schedule as follows:

1. Add a date line **Date (1-31)** to the **Date Zone** by Right Clicking in the **Date Zone** and selecting **Properties**:

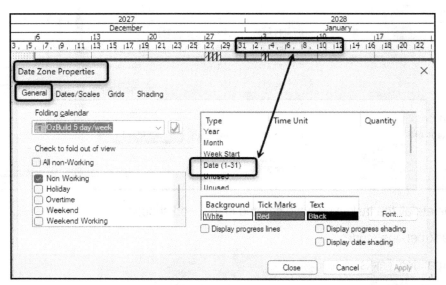

2. Display the **Elapsed Day** Gridline against all Date Zones,

3. Adjust the timescale to show all the day dates:

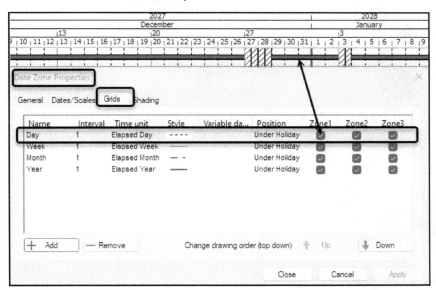

4. Slice the **Date Zone** twice by Right Clicking in the Timescale and selecting **Start New Scale Zone** on the end of 24 Dec 27 and 3 Jan 2028,

5. Then adjust each zone to a different scale:

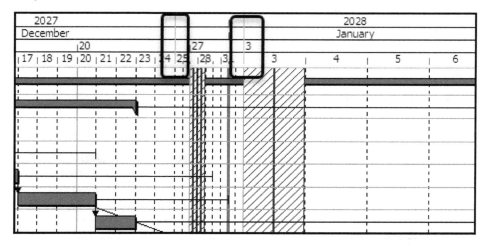

6. Remove the Time Zones by Right Clicking in the Timescale on the new Time Zones and selecting **Remove This Scale Zone**:

7. Select the **Date Zone Properties**, **General** tab, ensure the **Folding calendar** is the **OzBuild 5 day/week** and hide **All non-Working** time, you will see the Non-Work days are hidden:

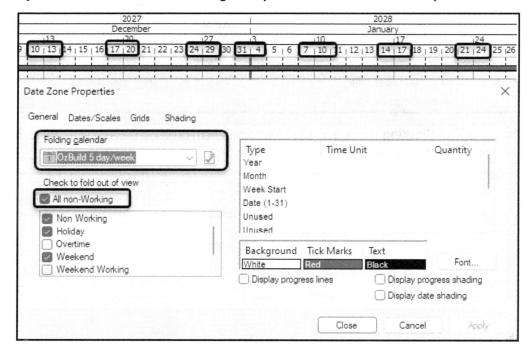

8. Now unclick all **Check fold out of view** options:

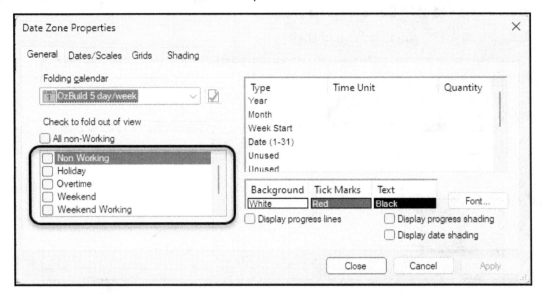

9. You will see that all work and non work times are dispalyed and critical relationships are not vertical:

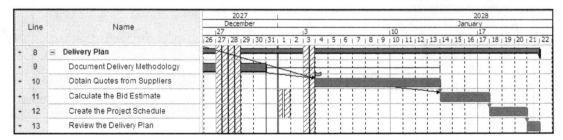

10. Check the **Non Working** check box, this hides times from 00:00 to 08:00 and 17:00 to 24:00.
11. Driving relationships are now vertical:

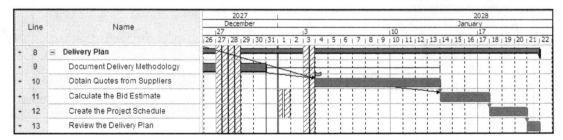

12. Check the **Holiday**, this will hide Holidays for the OzBuild 5 day/week calendar tasks but not the Saturday Holiday for the OzBuild 6 day/week calendar tasks because the folding calendar is the OzBuild 5 day/week calendar:

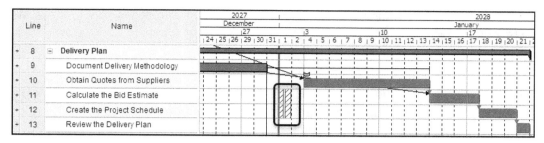

13. Uncheck **Holiday** and check **Weekend** to hide the weekends:

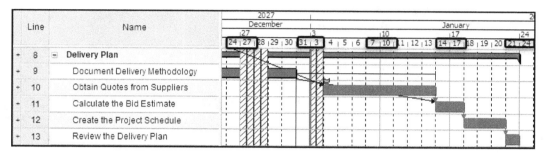

14. Use the Critical, Free Float and Total Float buttons to hde and display these bars:

15. Add the **Calendar** column and some other coumns such as Predecessors by right clicking on a heading and selecting **Add Column**, **Date**, **Calendar**:

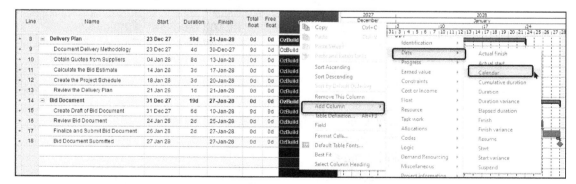

16. Remove the Columns.

17. Save your project.

Workshop 10 - Code Libraries

Background
We want to issue reports for comment by management by assigning responsibility to the activities and producing reports for each person.

Assignment
1. Creating a Responsibility Code,
    - Click on the **Open the Library Explorer** button to open the **Library Explorer**,
    - Add a **Responsibility** Code Library, and
    - Add three Codes with different display formatting for each code:
        - Angela Lowe - Purchasing
        - Carol Peterson - Bid Manager
        - Scott Morrison - Engineering

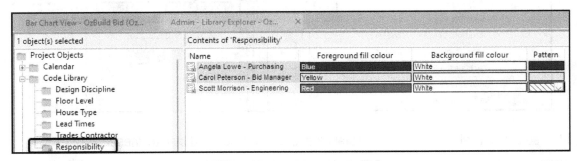

2. Assign the Responsibilities in the table below by clicking on the bars and dragging from the **Project View** or adding the **Task Responsibility** column:

ID	Task Name	Responsibility
1	**Bid for Facility Extension**	
2	**Technical Specification**	
3	Approval to Bid	
4	Determine Installation Requirements	Scott Morrison - Engineering
5	Create Technical Specification	Scott Morrison - Engineering
6	Identify Supplier Components	Angela Lowe - Purchasing
7	Validate Technical Specification	Scott Morrison - Engineering
8	**Delivery Plan**	
9	Document Delivery Methodology	Scott Morrison - Engineering
10	Obtain Quotes from Suppliers	Angela Lowe - Purchasing
11	Calculate the Bid Estimate	Scott Morrison - Engineering
12	Create the Project Schedule	Carol Peterson - Bid Manager
13	Review the Delivery Plan	Carol Peterson - Bid Manager
14	**Bid Document**	
15	Create Draft of Bid Document	Carol Peterson - Bid Manager
16	Review Bid Document	Carol Peterson - Bid Manager
17	Finalize and Submit Bid Document	Carol Peterson - Bid Manager
18	Bid Document Submitted	

3. Click **Yes** when you receive the message below:

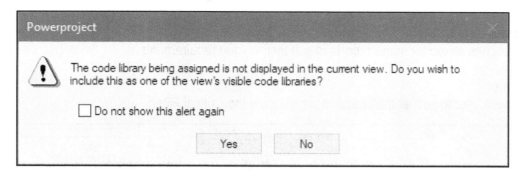

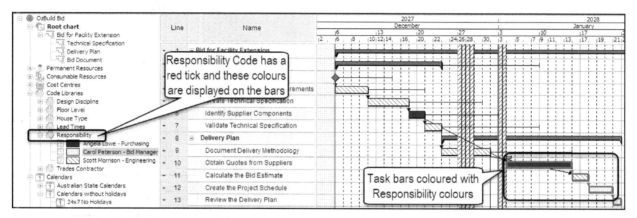

4. Now select **View**, **View Data** group, **Filter**, select **Which Code?** and produce a report for each responsible person:

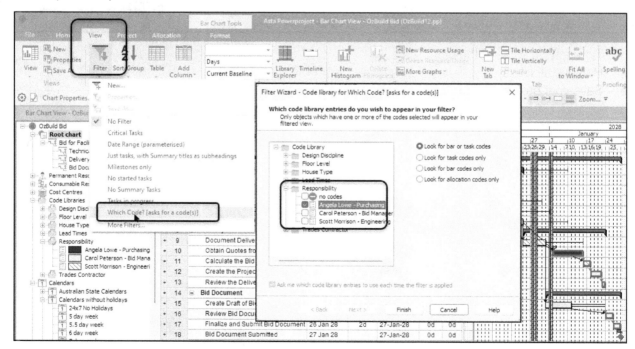

5. Remove all filters and any additional columns you have added, such as Responsibility and Calendar.
6. Save your **OzBuild Bid** project.

Workshop 11 – Filters

Background
Management has asked for some reports to suit their unique requirements.

Assignment
1. They would like to see all the critical tasks so apply the Critical Filter:

Line	Name	Start	Duration	Finish	Total float	Free float
1	Bid for Facility Extension	06 Dec 27	36d	27-Jan-28	0d	0d
2	Delivery Plan	23 Dec 27	19d	21-Jan-28	0d	0d
3	Obtain Quotes from Suppliers	04 Jan 28	8d	13-Jan-28	0d	0d
4	Calculate the Bid Estimate	14 Jan 28	3d	17-Jan-28	0d	0d
5	Create the Project Schedule	18 Jan 28	3d	20-Jan-28	0d	0d
6	Review the Delivery Plan	21 Jan 28	1d	21-Jan-28	0d	0d
7	Bid Document	31 Dec 27	19d	27-Jan-28	0d	0d
8	Review Bid Document	24 Jan 28	2d	25-Jan-28	0d	0d
9	Finalize and Submit Bid Document	26 Jan 28	2d	27-Jan-28	0d	0d
10	Bid Document Submitted	27 Jan 28		27-Jan-28	0d	0d

2. Now filter on Angela Lowes tasks using the **Which Code** filter.

Line	Name	Start	Duration	Finish	Total float	Free float
1	Bid for Facility Extension	06 Dec 27	36d	27-Jan-28	0d	0d
2	Technical Specification	06 Dec 27	13d	22-Dec-27	9d	0d
3	Identify Supplier Components	17 Dec 27	2d	20-Dec-27	7d	0d
4	Delivery Plan	23 Dec 27	19d	21-Jan-28	0d	0d
5	Obtain Quotes from Suppliers	04 Jan 28	8d	13-Jan-28	0d	0d

3. Try applying some of the other filters,
4. Remove all filters,
5. Save your project.

Workshop 12 - Organizing Tasks Using Group and Sort

Background
Having completed the schedule, you want to report the project schedule with different views.

Assignment
Create a Sort/Group to group the tasks by Responsibility:
1. From the **View** tab, select **Sort/Group**,
2. Click on **New**,
3. Enter a name for this sort, e.g. **Responsibility**,
4. Do not select a category for this sort,
5. In the Type column, select **Task**,
6. In the Attribute column select **Responsibility**,

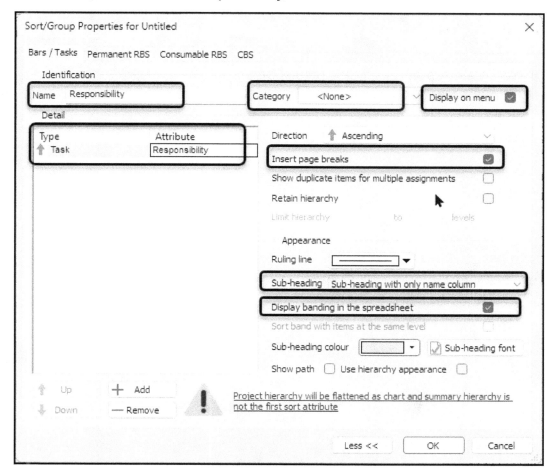

7. Tick Insert page break to have a page break at the bottom of each set of data. This will allow you to print each set of data on a separate page,
8. The Sub-heading drop down allows you to choose how you want the summary heading to be displayed, select **Subheading with only name column**,
9. Change the **Sub-heading font** to Ariel Bold 10.
10. Click OK to apply the sort,

---

11. Apply the **Task Only** filter, by selecting **Filter**, **More Filters...** to remove the summary tasks and Milestones:

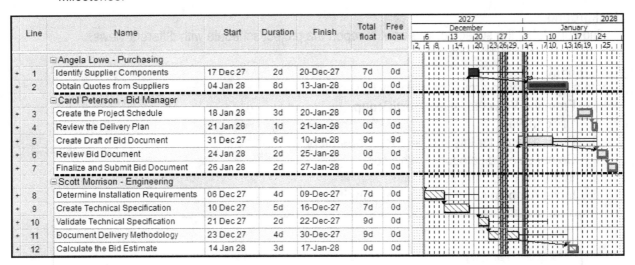

Line	Name	Start	Duration	Finish	Total float	Free float
	⊟ Angela Lowe - Purchasing					
1	Identify Supplier Components	17 Dec 27	2d	20-Dec-27	7d	0d
2	Obtain Quotes from Suppliers	04 Jan 28	8d	13-Jan-28	0d	0d
	⊟ Carol Peterson - Bid Manager					
3	Create the Project Schedule	18 Jan 28	3d	20-Jan-28	0d	0d
4	Review the Delivery Plan	21 Jan 28	1d	21-Jan-28	0d	0d
5	Create Draft of Bid Document	31 Dec 27	6d	10-Jan-28	9d	9d
6	Review Bid Document	24 Jan 28	2d	25-Jan-28	0d	0d
7	Finalize and Submit Bid Document	26 Jan 28	2d	27-Jan-28	0d	0d
	⊟ Scott Morrison - Engineering					
8	Determine Installation Requirements	06 Dec 27	4d	09-Dec-27	7d	0d
9	Create Technical Specification	10 Dec 27	5d	16-Dec-27	7d	0d
10	Validate Technical Specification	21 Dec 27	2d	22-Dec-27	9d	0d
11	Document Delivery Methodology	23 Dec 27	4d	30-Dec-27	9d	0d
12	Calculate the Bid Estimate	14 Jan 28	3d	17-Jan-28	0d	0d

12. Remove the Group and by selecting **Natural Order**
13. Remover the Filter,
14. Save your file.

Workshop 13 – Printing

Background
We want to issue a report for comment by management.

Assignment
1. Apply the **Bar Chart View** and remove any additional columns you have added so there are only the Line, Name, Start, Duration, Finish Total Float and Free Float columns displayed.
2. Select **File**, **Print**, **Options**.
3. Select A3 Landscape, or paper size that your country usually uses,
4. Select the Boarder file **CHT-A3L.B: A3 Landscape PowerDraw Generated** if available, or a boarder to suit your selected paper size:

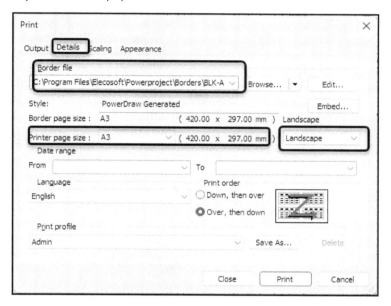

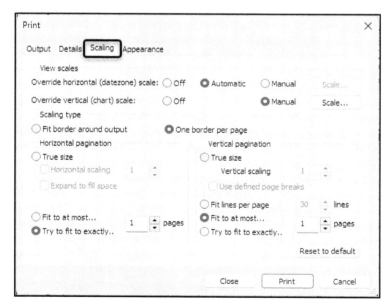

5. View the result:

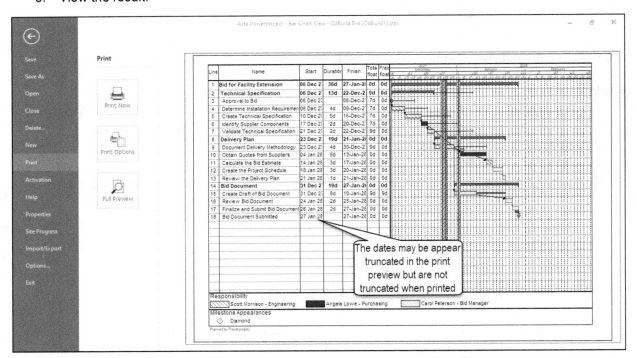

Workshop 14 - Setting a Baseline

Background
It is at the end of the first week you have to update the schedule to report progress and slippage.

Assignment
Open your **OzBuild Bid** project file and complete the following steps:

1. Set the Baseline for all the tasks on your project using the **Project, Properties** group, **Baseline Manager, New…** command and give the Baseline a name of **Contract Baseline**, and accept all the defaults

2. Apply the **Progress View** by selecting **View, Views** group, **View** and select **Progress View** from the drop-down list.

3. If the tasks are all rolled up the select **Show To Level** and select **All Levels**.

4. You will now have two views open and two tabs at the top of the Gannt Chart.

5. Each will require the baseline to be displayed selecting **Format, Format** group, **Format Bar Chart**, select the **Baselines** tab and check the box **Check to show for…** to display the baseline bars. At this point in time both the Contract and Current Baseline will be the same:

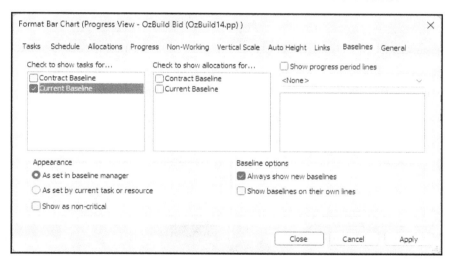

6. You should see the Baseline Bars below the current schedule, but your column formats may be different, but may be reformatted using the **Format Cells** command:

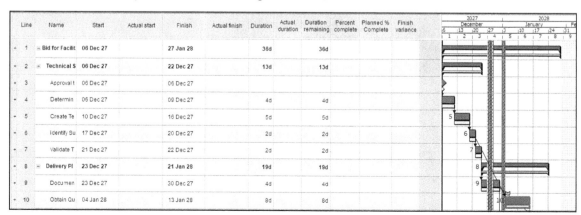

Workshop 15 - Updating an Unsourced Project

1. In this workshop we will only use one **Report Date** and use the **Progress View**.
2. Open the **Project View** by clicking on the **Project View** button on the **Quick Access Toolbar**,
3. Open the **Progress Period Properties for Project Report Date** form and change the **Project Report Dates to** 13 December 2027:

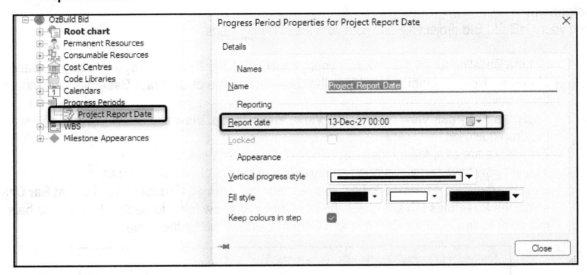

4. Open the **Format Bar Chart** form, select the **Progress** tab and ensure the boxes as per below are checked:

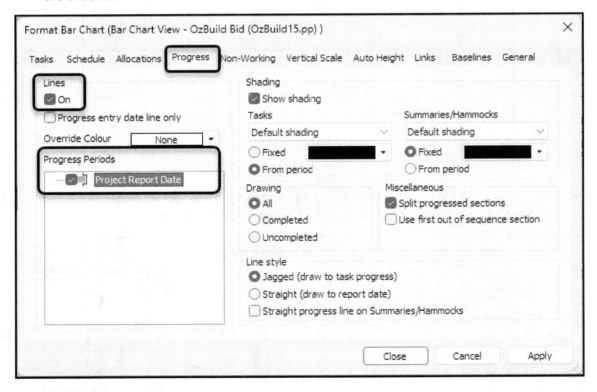

5. Select the **Baseline** tab and ensure the **Current Baseline** is displayed, this will be the same as the Contract Baseline at this point in time:

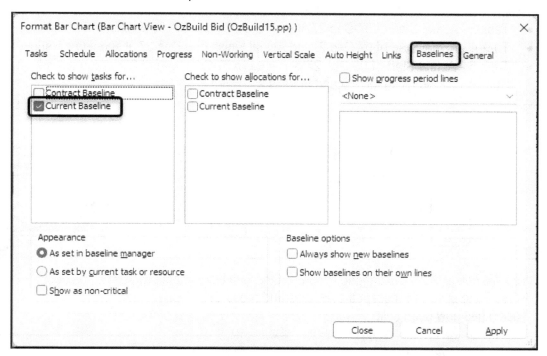

6. You should now see a Jagged Report Line and the Planned % Complete has been calculated:

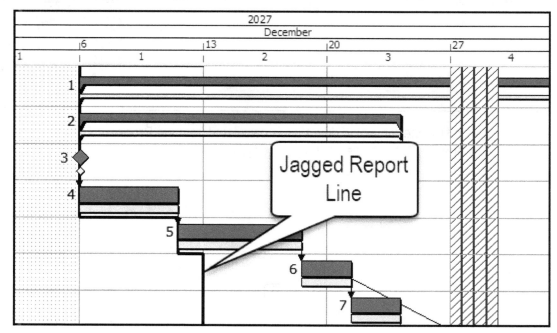

7. Expand the time scale as required to see the detail.
8. Apply the **Progress – with a baseline** table and ensure your columns are as per below.

Line	Name	Start	Actual start	Finish	Actual finish	Duration	Actual duration	Duration remaining	Percent complete	Planned % Complete	Finish variance

9. For clarity add the Grids for Elapsed Days and Date Zone time units of Day (1-31).
10. Select the **Root chart** and update the following tasks using the table below. Enter the data in the exact order below against the detail tasks only:
    - Task 3 - Actual Start of 07-Dec-27, it should also show 100 % against the Milestones,
    - Task 4 - Actual Start of 07-Dec-27and Actual Finish of 9-Dec-27, it should now show 100%,
    - Task 5 - Actual Start of 09-Dec-27 and enter a % Complete of 20%. You will see the Actual Duration is calculated for you and there is a Jagged Progress Line:

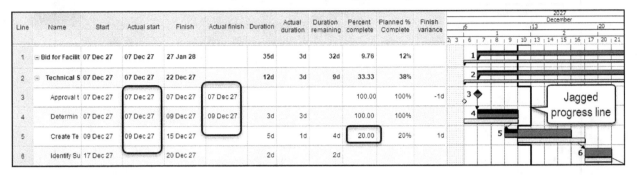

11. You will notice there is a Jagged Progress Line with incomplete progress in the past,
12. Press F9 to schedule, accept the defaults and press OK.
13. Task 5 has now been split.

Line	Name	Start	Actual start	Finish	Actual finish	Duration	Actual duration	Duration remaining	Percent complete	Planned % Complete	Finish variance
1	Bid for Facilit	07 Dec 27	07 Dec 27	27 Jan 28		35d	4d	31d	9.76	12%	
2	Technical S	07 Dec 27	07 Dec 27	22 Dec 27		12d	4d	8d	33.33	38%	
3	Approval t	07 Dec 27	07 Dec 27	07 Dec 27	07 Dec 27				100.00	100%	-1d
4	Determin	07 Dec 27	07 Dec 27	09 Dec 27	09 Dec 27	3d	3d		100.00	100%	
5	Create Te	09 Dec 27	09 Dec 27	16 Dec 27		5d	1d	4d	20.00	20%	
6	Identify Su	17 Dec 27		20 Dec 27		2d		2d			

14. At this point in time the remaining d6uration is calculated from the **Progress Date**.
15. Task 5 - change the **Duration remaining** to 6 days and reschedule.

Line	Name	Start	Actual start	Finish	Actual finish	Duration	Actual duration	Duration remaining	Percent complete	Planned % Complete	Finish variance
1	Bid for Facilit	07 Dec 27	07 Dec 27	27 Jan 28		35d	4d	31d	9.30	12%	
2	Technical S	07 Dec 27	07 Dec 27	24 Dec 27		14d	4d	10d	28.57	38%	-2d
3	Approval t	07 Dec 27	07 Dec 27	07 Dec 27	07 Dec 27				100.00	100%	-1d
4	Determin	07 Dec 27	07 Dec 27	09 Dec 27	09 Dec 27	3d	3d		100.00	100%	
5	Create Te	09 Dec 27	09 Dec 27	20 Dec 27		7d	1d	6d	14.29	20%	-2d
6	Identify Su	21 Dec 27		22 Dec 27		2d		2d			-2d

16. **Note:** there is no change in the end date of the project as there is enough Float to absorb the delay.

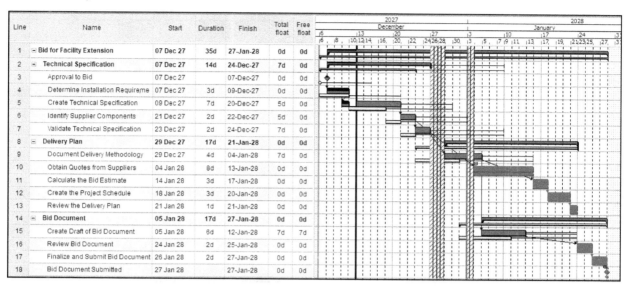

Line	Name	Start	Duration	Finish	Total float	Free float
1	⊟ Bid for Facility Extension	07 Dec 27	35d	27-Jan-28	0d	0d
2	⊟ Technical Specification	07 Dec 27	14d	24-Dec-27	7d	0d
3	Approval to Bid	07 Dec 27		07-Dec-27	0d	0d
4	Determine Installation Requireme	07 Dec 27	3d	09-Dec-27	0d	0d
5	Create Technical Specification	09 Dec 27	7d	20-Dec-27	5d	0d
6	Identify Supplier Components	21 Dec 27	2d	22-Dec-27	5d	0d
7	Validate Technical Specification	23 Dec 27	2d	24-Dec-27	7d	0d
8	⊟ Delivery Plan	29 Dec 27	17d	21-Jan-28	0d	0d
9	Document Delivery Methodology	29 Dec 27	4d	04-Jan-28	7d	0d
10	Obtain Quotes from Suppliers	04 Jan 28	8d	13-Jan-28	0d	0d
11	Calculate the Bid Estimate	14 Jan 28	3d	17-Jan-28	0d	0d
12	Create the Project Schedule	18 Jan 28	3d	20-Jan-28	0d	0d
13	Review the Delivery Plan	21 Jan 28	1d	21-Jan-28	0d	0d
14	⊟ Bid Document	05 Jan 28	17d	27-Jan-28	0d	0d
15	Create Draft of Bid Document	05 Jan 28	6d	12-Jan-28	7d	7d
16	Review Bid Document	24 Jan 28	2d	25-Jan-28	0d	0d
17	Finalize and Submit Bid Document	26 Jan 28	2d	27-Jan-28	0d	0d
18	Bid Document Submitted	27 Jan 28		27-Jan-28	0d	0d

17. Save your OzBuild Bid project.

Workshop 16 - Library Explorer

1. Display the **Library Explorer** and open the **Show Libraries** form.

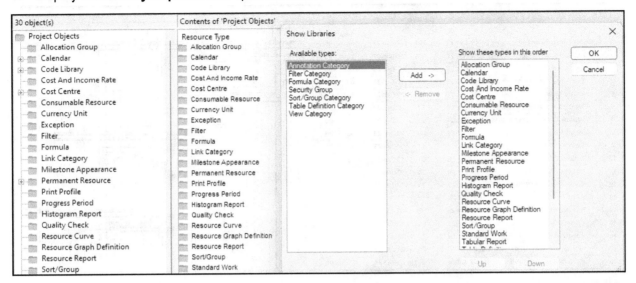

2. Ensure only Category fields are NOT displayed and they are therefore listed under **Available Types**,
3. Reorder the displayed heading alphabetically,
4. Close the **Show Libraries** form,
5. Check your results and then close the Library Explorer.

Course Agenda and PowerPoint Slides

Day 1 - Create an Unresourced Project

1. Introduction to Asta Powerproject and Creating a Project
2. Navigation and Setting Options
3. Calendars
4. Tasks and Milestones
5. Summary Tasks
6. Linking Tasks to create a Critical Path Schedule and Reschedule
7. Constraints
8. Other Task Types

Day 2 – Formatting, Reports and Updating an Unresourced Project

9. Formatting the Display
10. Code Libraries
11. Filters
12. Organising Tasks using Group and Sorts
13. Printing and Reports
14. Baselines
15. Updating an Unresourced Project
16. Library Explorer
17. User Definable Fields and WBS.

EASTWOOD HARRIS PTY LTD.

NEW Pickie Needed

Page 1

1

EASTWOOD HARRIS PTY LTD.

Welcome to the
**Create and Update an
Unresourced Project
using
Elecosoft (Asta) Powerproject
Version 17**
training course

Page 2

2

1

EASTWOOD HARRIS PTY LTD.

Administration

- Evacuation and First Aid,
- Facilities, timings and meals,
- Mobile phones & emails,
- Introductions:
  - Your name,
  - The types of projects you are involved in,
  - Your experience in scheduling software, and
  - What you intend to do with the software after the course,
- Course attendance sheet.

Copyright Eastwood Harris Pty Ltd 2023

Page 3

3

EASTWOOD HARRIS PTY LTD.

Required background to attend this course

To attend this course you are expected to:

- Understand how projects are managed and the project management process required to run projects,
- Understand how to use PCs and the operating system,
- A basic understanding of Critical Path concepts, including how the forward and backward pass calculate Early Dates, Late Dates, the Critical Path and Float,
- Experience in using project planning and scheduling software such as Microsoft Project or Primavera P6, etc. would be beneficial but not essential.

Copyright Eastwood Harris Pty Ltd 2023

Page 4

4

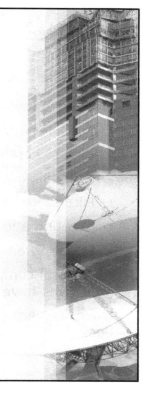

EASTWOOD HARRIS PTY LTD.

Background Reading

There are many books on the market that give guidance on the creation and updating of project schedules:

- *PMBOK® Guide*
- PRINCE2
- AACE International publications,
  - Total Cost Management and
  - The Recommended Practices, relevant ones are listed on the next slide

5

EASTWOOD HARRIS PTY LTD.

ID	TITLE
14R-90	Responsibility and Required Skills for a Project Planning and Scheduling Professional
20R-98	Project Code of Accounts
21R-98	Project Code of Accounts – As Applied in Engineering, Procurement, and Construction for the Process Industries
23R-02	Identification of Activities
24R-03	Developing Activity Logic
27R-03	Schedule Classification System
32R-04	Determining Activity Durations
37R-06	Schedule Levels of Detail—As Applied in Engineering, Procurement, and Construction
38R-06	Documenting the Schedule Basis
39R-06	Project Planning – As Applied in Engineering and Construction for Capital Projects
45R-08	Scheduling Claims Protection Methods
48R-06	Schedule Constructability Review
49R-06	Identifying the Critical Path
52R-06	Prospective Time Impact Analysis – As Applied in Construction
61R-10	Schedule Design – As Applied in Engineering, Procurement, and Construction
70R-12	Principles of Schedule Contingency Management – As Applied in Engineering, Procurement and Construction
78R-13	Original Baseline Schedule Review - As Applied in Engineering, Procurement, and Construction
82R-13	Earned Value Management (EVM) Overview and Recommended Practices Consistent with EIA-748-C
84R-13	Planning and Accounting for Adverse Weather
89R-16	Management Summary Schedule
91R-16	Schedule Development
92R-17	Analyzing Near-Critical Paths

6

EASTWOOD HARRIS PTY LTD.

Course Objectives

This objectives of this course are to teach participants:

- The user interface,
- How to create a project,
- Scheduling projects without resources,
- Filters, Views, Sorts and Printing,
- Creating and assigning a baseline and
- Updating an un-resourced project,

Successful completion of all the course workshops will confirm that the objectives have been met,

Note: Powerproject has a large amount of functionality and this course does not cover all aspects of the software. Please refer to the help files for a more detailed understanding of the functions not covered.

Copyright Eastwood Harris Pty Ltd 2023

Page 7

7

EASTWOOD HARRIS PTY LTD.

Course Conduct

- This course is instructor lead,
- The instructor will demonstrate the software with a combination of PowerPoint presentations and live software demonstrations,
- Most topics are reinforced by workshops,
- The manual is yours to take away,
- Take any notes,
- Ask any questions,
- The screen dumps in these slides are a mixture of Version 16 and Version 17.

Copyright Eastwood Harris Pty Ltd 2023

Page 8

8

EASTWOOD HARRIS PTY LTD.

Course Agenda – Day 1

Create an Unresourced Project

1. Introduction to Powerproject and Creating a project
2. Navigation and Setting Options
3. Calendars
4. Tasks and Milestones
5. Summary Tasks
6. Linking Tasks to create a Critical Path Schedule
7. Constraints.

9

EASTWOOD HARRIS PTY LTD.

Course Agenda – Day 2

Formatting, Printing and Reports

8. Other Task Types
9. Formatting the Display
10. Code Libraries
11. Filters
12. Organising Tasks using Sort and Groups
13. Printing and Reports

Updating an Unresourced Project

14. Baselines
15. Updating an Unresourced Project
16. User Definable Fields and WBS.

10

EASTWOOD HARRIS PTY LTD.

Downloading Workshop Files

- The student workshop instructions, completed workshop files and Quick Access Toolbar may be download from this web site,
- The completed student workshop files and Quick Access Toolbar may also be download from **www.eh.com.au**,
- The student workshop instructions are a pdf file that you may follow to complete the student workshops,
- The completed workshops may be opened to check your answers and they are in ZIP file that will require unzipping before opening with Powerproject,
- A simple method of unzipping the files is to double click on the ZIP file to open it and then click and drag the files inside the ZIP file to your desktop,
- The Quick Access Toolbar should be imported and instructions will be given at the appropriate time.

Copyright Eastwood Harris Pty Ltd 2023

Page 11

11

EASTWOOD HARRIS PTY LTD.

1 - INTRODUCTION TO POWERPROJECT

- Asta Powerproject was developed in the UK and is one of the oldest PC project scheduling software packages,
- Asta plc was purchase by Elecosoft plc and the term Asta is no longer used by Elecosoft,
- It is very similar in structure to Microsoft Project and Tables, Views, Grouping and Filters have similar functions,
- It has greater functionality than P6 or Microsoft Project which makes the learning curve longer than for other products,
- P6 and Microsoft Project were developed for IT and Business projects and are missing functions desirable on construction projects that are available with Powerproject,
- Powerproject was developed for the construction industry and is more suitable for building and construction projects,
- It uses some different terminology to US products.

Copyright Eastwood Harris Pty Ltd 2023

Page 12

12

EASTWOOD HARRIS PTY LTD.

Powerproject Products

Elecosoft has the following main products and many add on software packages:

- **Powerproject**, the main scheduling engine,
- **Project Viewer**, a free viewer where a schedule may be opened and viewed but not modified,
- **4D Planning** by importing your 3D CAD model,
- **Site Progress Mobile**, an app allowing users to record the progress of their project on their mobile phone,
- **Asta Enterprise** allows multiple users to view projects that are updated in real time
- **Powerproject Vision** a hosted service that allows all users to create a new project from templates and access the latest version of the project program from any location,
- **Asta Connect** a solves the challenges of short-term, on-site planning, collaboration and daily activities progress by connecting project teams with the overall master construction schedule and capturing commitments.

Copyright Eastwood Harris Pty Ltd 2023

13

EASTWOOD HARRIS PTY LTD.

Powerproject Modes

Powerproject may be run in several modes:

- Single user opening one Powerproject file,
- Multi users opening one Powerproject file,
- Multiple projects and multiple users accessing one database,
- When multiple users are opening a project then security is set at user and task level with real time updates for other users.

Copyright Eastwood Harris Pty Ltd 2023

14

7

EASTWOOD HARRIS PTY LTD.

Powerproject Addon Software

Powerproject has a number of addons that users may download from the Powerproject support website at https://support.elecosoft.com/, some listed below:

- **Addon to move code library items into different libraries** which solves the issue multiple Code assignment to one task which may not be exported to P6,

- **XER Update addon for Primavera P6 baseline imports** to enable Powerproject to import a XER P6 Baseline,

- **Project Comparison** for comparing two projects for changes and forensic analysis,

- **Progress Tools** a collection of tools for examining, transferring or modifying progress,

- **Standard Data Exchange Format (SDEF) Exporter** for the US Military,

- **Predecessor / successor report addon**

- **Lean Construction Suite**

- **BidCon importer for Powerproject**

Copyright Eastwood Harris Pty Ltd 2023

Page 15

15

EASTWOOD HARRIS PTY LTD.

What is new in Powerproject Version 16 1/2

- A **Calculated Weight** field has been added to improve the way the overall percent complete has been calculated,

- Text formatting may now be retained with **Copy and Paste**,

- **Strikethrough** formatting may be applied to text,

- A new dialog box assists with problems when projects do not open,

- Improvements allowing the temporary removal of **Date Range Shading**,

- Introduction of **Date Zone** shading, plus the ability to not print date range shading on the Gantt Chart, say to save on ink,

- Copy and Paste date range shading between Views,

- **Group and Sort Subheading Calendar** now uses the task calendar when all tasks in the subheading are assigned the same calendar,

- Import of P6 schedules Summary bar calendars assigned as per the above.

Copyright Eastwood Harris Pty Ltd 2023

Page 16

16

EASTWOOD HARRIS PTY LTD.

What is new in Powerproject Version 16 2/2

- Match and update code libraries when importing a P6 into a template so duplicate code libraries are not created,
- You may now specify where backups are stored,
- The ability to display the **Code Name** or the **Code Short Name** on Gantt Chart bars,
- **Progress periods** are now available as fields for formulae,
- Summary task Planned percent complete may be displayed as the distributed average for charts/summaries allowing a more accurate percent complete to be assigned against summary tasks,
- Special characters allowed in **User-Defined** fields allowing a better integration wit P6 and prevents duplication of data on import and export of projects to P6.

EASTWOOD HARRIS PTY LTD.

What is new in Powerproject Version 17

The following new Version 17 features covered in this course:

- **Autosave** in now available and operates in a similar way to Microsoft Project,
- A **Timeline View** which is similar to the Microsoft Project Timeline View is now available,
- Specify **Materials type** when recording **Task Work** details,

There is an article titled **What's New in Elecosoft (Asta) Powerproject Version 17** on www.eh.com.au which covers the remaining Version 17 new features that would be used in a single project environment,

- **View Tabs** may be assigned a colour enabling simpler identification of projects and views that are applied to projects,
- Tasks may be broken down into smaller steps called **Task Activities**, similar to Steps in Primavera P6.

EASTWOOD HARRIS PTY LTD.

Powerproject Terminology

Powerproject has some different terminology to US software:

Powerproject	P6 and Microsoft Project
Live project	Current project
Links	Relationships
Relationship, this is the relationship of detailed tasks to a summary task.	This is equivalent to P6 WBS levels and MPS Outline levels.
Block Linking	Chain Linking
Allocate Resource	Assign Resource
Allocation	Assignment
Date Zone	Timescale
Rulers	Gridlines
Report Date	Data Date – P6 Status Date – Microsoft Project
Imposed start	Project Start Date
Subheading - a description without a Gantt chart bar.	No equivalent.
Annotation	A graphic item added to the Gantt Chart.

Copyright Eastwood Harris Pty Ltd 2023

Page 19

19

EASTWOOD HARRIS PTY LTD.

Mouse Clicking and Copy and Paste

Powerproject follows many Microsoft Windows conventions:

- Left click will select an item,
- Double click will activate it,
- Right click opens a menu,
- Click and drag moves a cell or selects multiple items,
- Shift button allows selection of adjacent items,
- Control button allows selection of non-adjacent items,
- Copy and Paste. When copying from a spreadsheet you must select more than one cell in Powerproject before pasting. For example, if you select and copy 6 cells in a spreadsheet then if you select one cell in Powerproject all the data will be pasted into the one Powerproject cell. To paste into 6 cells you must select 2 or more cells in Powerproject before pasting. If you select 12 cells in Powerproject the data will be pasted twice. *Copyright Eastwood Harris Pty Ltd 2023*

Page 20

20

EASTWOOD HARRIS PTY LTD.

Undo and Redo

- The Powerproject **Undo** and **Redo** function does not operate on formatting functions, it only works on edits that affect the schedule calculations and schedule data,

- An **Undo** is not lost when a project is saved,

- All **Undos** are lost when a project is closed,

- A list of **Undos** is available from the dropdown list by the Undo icon:

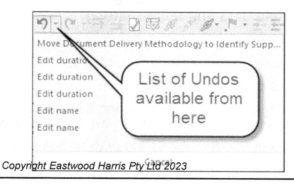

Move Document Delivery Methodology to Identify Supp...

Edit duration
Edit duration
Edit duration
Edit name
Edit name

List of Undos available from here

Copyright Eastwood Harris Pty Ltd 2023

Page 21

21

EASTWOOD HARRIS PTY LTD.

File Locations

- After opening Powerproject for the first time you will need to set the file locations to suit your requirements,

- To set the Powerproject directories select **File**, **Options**, **File Locations**:

- You will need to save your templates into the **Template** folder,

- Set your **Live** and **Baseline** file directory, these are best set as the same directory, so you do not missplace your Baseline files,

- **Notes:**

  - The **Baseline** directory was initially not used in Version 15 and then reinstated,

  - **Backup Files directory was** added in Version 16.

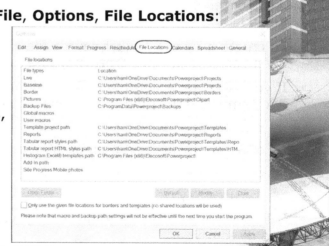

Copyright Eastwood Harris Pty Ltd 2024

Page 22

22

EASTWOOD HARRIS PTY LTD.

File Extensions

Powerproject projects have the following files extensions:

- Live projects (Current project) - *.pp
- Templates - *.pp
- Backup projects - *.bak
- Boarder files used when printing*.b
- Baselines - *.ppb, Baseline files are smaller than a Live project files because they only hold data and no formatting
- **Notes**
  - Version 14 and earlier read the baseline from a file in a *.ppb format,
  - Version 15.1 would only save the baseline as part of the current project,
  - Version 15.2 gave users the option of saving a baseline as a separate file like earlier versions in *.ppb format or as part of the current project file,
  - Version 16 has a new file format and will update files when they are opened.

Page 23   *Copyright Eastwood Harris Pty Ltd 2023*

23

EASTWOOD HARRIS PTY LTD.

Creating Templates

- Corporate templates are essential when using Powerproject and should include items such as Codes, Calendars, Views, Filters, Border files, Reports and sample task sets,
- To create a Template just save a file in the Template directory that has been selected in **File**, **Options**, **File Locations**, **Template** project path,
- If you have been upgrading from earlier versions of Powerproject you may find templates in several locations which are all read by Powerproject:
  - c:\program files\
  - c:\program files (x86)\ on 64-bit machines
  - c:\programdata\
  - the users My Documents folder,
- It is recommended that you clean up your templates so they only reside in one directory:

Page 24   *Copyright Eastwood Harris Pty Ltd 2023*

24

EASTWOOD HARRIS PTY LTD.

Template Location History

- Powerproject templates are saved in different locations for compatibility reasons:

- Windows XP which does not have newer security restrictions are in the c:\program files\ since it is accessible by all users on the machine,

- With Windows Vista, Microsoft introduced the new security rules preventing user access to c:\program files\ and then Template were set to:

  - Saved in c:\programdata\ if required by all users, or

  - Save in the users My Documents folder if only required by the individual user,

- You may end up with templates in several locations and they are all read by Powerproject irrespective of your **File**, **Locations** setting,

- If you wish to delete all Powerproject templates you may need to look in all these locations.

Page 25

Copyright Eastwood Harris Pty Ltd 2023

25

EASTWOOD HARRIS PTY LTD.

Powerproject Properties Forms

- Powerproject has a number of Properties forms and therefore when you open a Properties form you need to be aware of what Properties form you are opening,

- For example there are:

  - **Date Zone Properties**
  - **Chart Properties**
  - **Calendar Properties**
  - **Filter Properties**
  - **Sort and Group Properties**

- Therefore when you are in the **Date Zone** and right click and select **Properties** you will open the form.

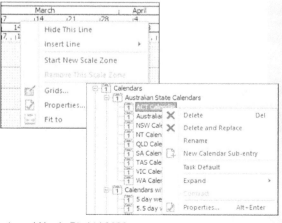

Page 26

Copyright Eastwood Harris Pty Ltd 2023

26

EASTWOOD HARRIS PTY LTD.

System Date Format

- The date format displayed in Powerproject dialogue boxes, such as the **Start Date** in the **Chart Properties** form, is adopted from your **System Short Date** format,

- You may change your **System Short Date** from **Start**, **Settings**, **Time and Language** and this will affect dates in many apps such as File Explorer etc.,

- The workshops display the format of dd-MMM-yy and display dates in this format: 31-Dec-21,

- Thus, people in the US (that use the format mm-dd-yy, 12-31-21) and most Western countries (that use the format of dd-mm-yy, 31-12-21) will all understand the date formats used in the workshops,

- The formatting of dates of columns is covered in the Formatting section of this course.

Page 27

27

EASTWOOD HARRIS PTY LTD.

Creating a Project

- Templates are used to make creating a new project as simple as possible. Template should contain information that you may wish to use regularly such as tables, code libraries, filters and many more items,

- Select **File**, **New**,

- Select a template on which to base your project e.g. Construction Template,

- Enter the project details,

- **Note**: It is very important to create your own organisations templates to save your schedulers from creating the same **Filters**, **Calendars**, **Currencies** and **Views** over and over again.

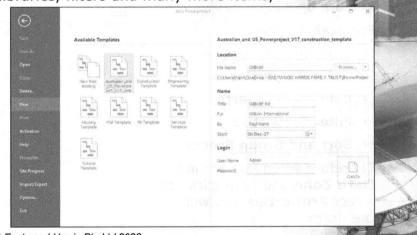

Page 28

28

EASTWOOD HARRIS PTY LTD.

Opening an existing project

To open a protect:

- Select **File**, **Open**,
- Use the applicable option from this form,
- There is a new option to use **Powerproject Vision**.

EASTWOOD HARRIS PTY LTD.

Importing a Microsoft Project, SureTrak or Primavera P6 Project

- Powerproject will import all of these project file types from the **File**, **Import** command:
- Microsoft Project files must be saved in XML format unless you have Microsoft Project loaded and then files in MPP format may be imported,
- SureTrak in STX format,
- P6 in XER or XML format,
- **Note:** The projects created by different software will often calculate differently and will often display different dates, costs or units.

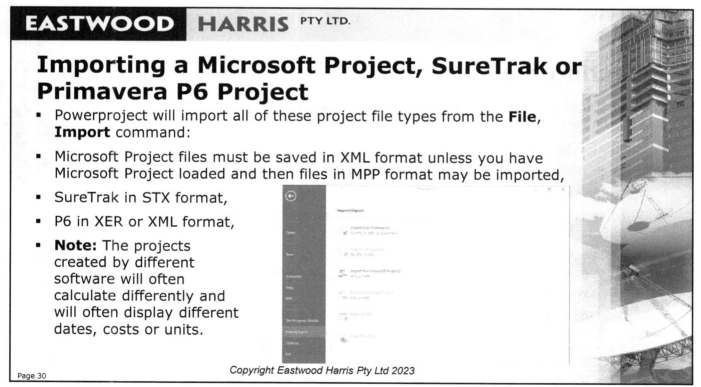

15

EASTWOOD HARRIS PTY LTD.

Changing the Project Start Date

- The start date of a selected project may be changed by:

  - Selecting **File**, **Properties**, or **File**, **Properties**, **Advanced Properties**,

  - Change the **Imposed start** to the new project start date and click **Close**:

  - The date format displayed in Powerproject dialogue boxes, such as the Start Date in the **File**, **New form**, is adopted from your System Short Date format,

- **Note:** If your project does not move when you have changed your Imposed Start then check your **Report Date**.

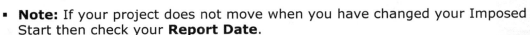

Properties for Bid for Facility Extension   ×

Properties   Fields

Details

Name   Bid for Facility Extension

Short name   BEF   Status   Normal

For   Wilson International   By   Paul Harris

Default tab colour ▭ ▾

Dates

Start date   02-Dec-21 10:26:26   Duration   56ed 6.56eh

Finish date   27-Jan-22 17:00   Duration unit Elapsed Days ∨

Imposed start ☑ 06-Dec-21 00:00   Imposed finish ☐ 02-Jan-24 00:00

Page 31

Copyright Eastwood Harris Pty Ltd 2023

31

EASTWOOD HARRIS PTY LTD.

Selecting the currency

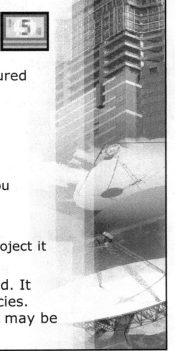

- Powerproject templates loaded with the software are often configured with UK Pounds as the currency,

- To change the currency to a different currency:

  - Open the project that you will be working with,

  - Display the **Currencies** in the **Library Explorer**,

  - If the currency you require does not exist then add the currency you require or rename an existing currency,

  - Assign your **Currency** to your project, and

  - Save your new project as a template, so when you create a new project it will have the correct **Currency**,

- **Note:** One currency is the **Base currency** and may not be deleted. It has a ⑤ icon and is used to calculate the rates of all other currencies. This and one other system currency may not be deleted, but they may be renamed.

Page 32

Copyright Eastwood Harris Pty Ltd 2023

32

Showing the currency in the Library Explorer

- Select **View**, **Library Explorer**, to open the **Library Explorer** in a new window,

- Right click in the bottom left hand window and select **Show Libraries...**,

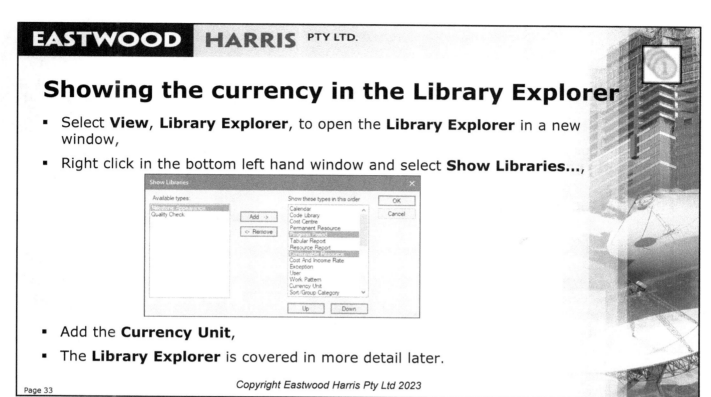

- Add the **Currency Unit**,

- The **Library Explorer** is covered in more detail later.

33

Creating a new currency

- Click on the **Currency Unit** in the **Library Explorer**,

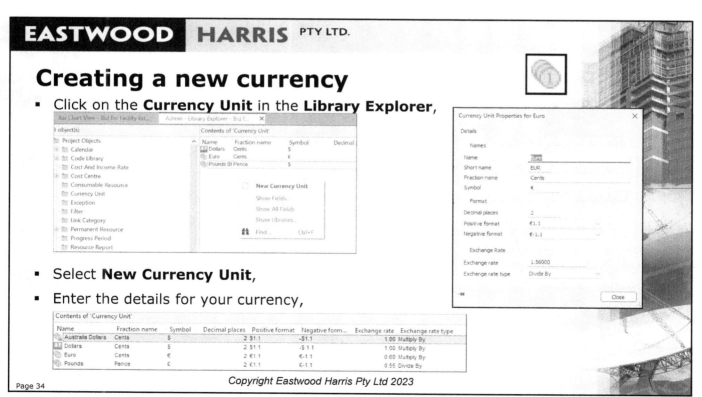

- Select **New Currency Unit**,

- Enter the details for your currency,

34

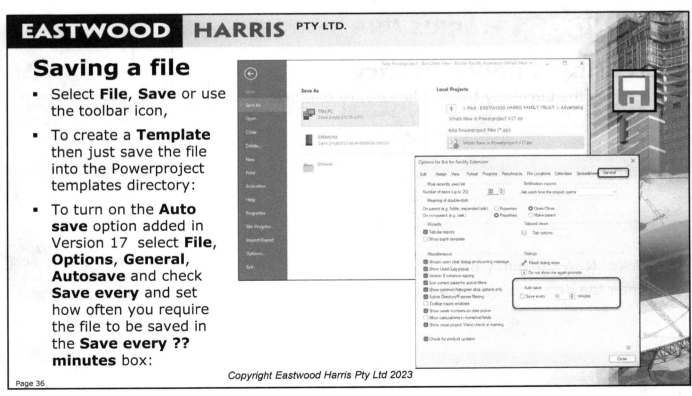

Setting the default currency

- Select **File**, **Options**, **View** tab,

- Select your currency under **Default currency**,

- A template should be created with the **Default currency** set,

- An Australian and US dollar construction template is available at www.eh.com.au and select Software and Downloads.

Page 35

Copyright Eastwood Harris Pty Ltd 2023

35

Saving a file

- Select **File**, **Save** or use the toolbar icon,

- To create a **Template** then just save the file into the Powerproject templates directory:

- To turn on the **Auto save** option added in Version 17 select **File**, **Options**, **General**, **Autosave** and check **Save every** and set how often you require the file to be saved in the **Save every ?? minutes** box:

Page 36

Copyright Eastwood Harris Pty Ltd 2023

36

EASTWOOD HARRIS PTY LTD.

Powerproject File Versions

- Powerproject introduces new file formats at times,

- Version 16 and 17 have new formats and you need to save in an older version for users with earlier versions of the software,

- Older versions are automatically converted on opening,

- If you wish to share a project with a user with an earlier version of Powerproject then you will need to use the **File**, **Save As** option and select an earlier version:

Page 37

Copyright Eastwood Harris Pty Ltd 2023

37

EASTWOOD HARRIS PTY LTD.

Saving a file with a new name

- When a file is saved with a new name, the existing version is kept as last saved, and a new version is saved under the new name,

- Select **File**, **Save As**, or click on the **Save As** icon,

- Select the location and name for your file and press **Save**:

Page 38

Copyright Eastwood Harris Pty Ltd 2023

38

EASTWOOD HARRIS PTY LTD.

Closing a project

- Select **File**, **Close**,
- If the project has not been saved you will be prompted to save it, or
- You may also close a project by closing all the open windows by clicking on the **X** in the tab,

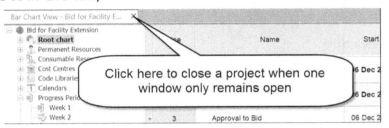

- When the last project tab is closed the project will be closed and you will be prompted to save the project.

Copyright Eastwood Harris Pty Ltd 2023

Page 39

39

EASTWOOD HARRIS PTY LTD.

Exiting Powerproject

- Select **File**, **Exit**,
- Powerproject will ask you to save a project when you close a project, or shutdown the software without saving the project:

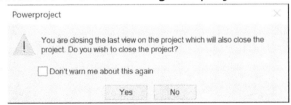

- The **File**, **Options**, **File Locations** has a location for the saving a backup file and these will be saved in this directory with a *.bak extension,
- To open a *.bak file just change the extension to *.PP.

Copyright Eastwood Harris Pty Ltd 2023

Page 40

40

EASTWOOD HARRIS PTY LTD.

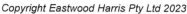

Powerproject Help

- Powerproject help is all web-based help is available by clicking on the Help button,

- UK support is through Elecosoft:
  Web: http://www.elecosoft.com/
  Tel: 01844 261609
  Email: support@elecosoft.com

- Australian support is available through Solid Support:
  Web: http://www.solidsupport.com.au/
  Tel: 02 9743 4666
  Email: helpdesk@solidsupport.com.au

- US support is available through Elecosoft LLC:
  Web: http://www.elecosoft.com/
  Tel: +1 855 553 2782
  Email: inquiries@elecosoft.com

Copyright Eastwood Harris Pty Ltd 2023

Page 41

41

EASTWOOD HARRIS PTY LTD.

Workshop 1 – Creating a Project

- You will create a new project from a template,

- A project template in *.pp format titled Australian and US Powerproject Version 17 construction template has been loaded on the Eastwood Harris web site at **www.eh.com.au Software Downloads** page that has a number of the issues with the UK templates resolved, including the default currency and calendar holidays,

- When you are watching a video training course then this template is available for download from the website you are watching the course,

- If you are from a country that uses the Dollar then you should download this file, save it in the Powerproject template directory and use this file,

- **Note:** This file has the UK calendars removed and the default Currency set to Dollars and cents with a $ symbol,

- You are welcome to use any other template, but your screen may not look the same as the ones in screen shots.

Copyright Eastwood Harris Pty Ltd 2023

Page 42

42

EASTWOOD HARRIS PTY LTD.

2 - NAVIGATION AND SETTING OPTIONS

- This module covers Powerproject screen and some of the navigation commands,
- The Powerproject screen is composed of a number of areas,
  - **Toolbars** – Contains shortcut buttons to menu functions,
  - **Barchart** – Information on your project in graphic form,
  - **Spreadsheet** – Information on your project in table form,
  - **Project View** – A window enabling the assignment of resources, calendars and codes by click and dragging,
  - **Object Edit Toolbar** – Used to edit tasks and/or links in the Gantt Chart,
  - **Date zone** – Shows the dates over the Gantt Chart,
  - **Properties View** – Allows you to edit the properties of a selected object.

Page 43

43

EASTWOOD HARRIS PTY LTD.

Page 44

44

Screen Bands

- The default setting is with bands shown across the screen and applies to all projects on a computer:

- These bands may be removed, see next slide:

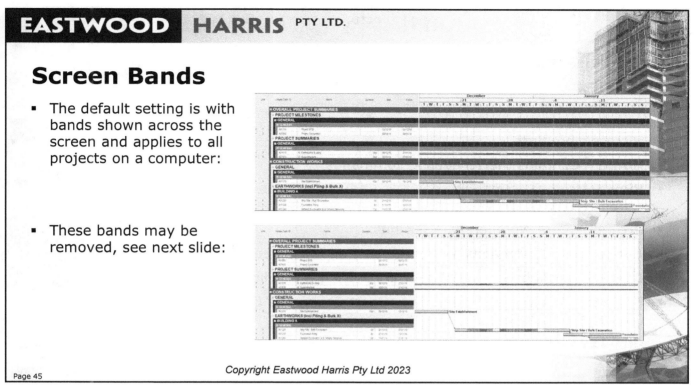

Removing Screen Bands

- To remove the thick coloured bands running across the screen,

- Select **File**, **Options**, **View** tab and uncheck **Show sort bands in the bar chart**,

- This is a system setting and applies to all projects you open.

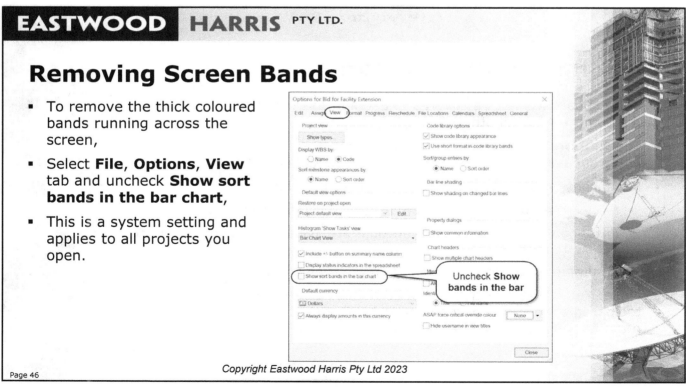

Uncheck **Show bands in the bar**

EASTWOOD HARRIS PTY LTD.

The Ribbon toolbar

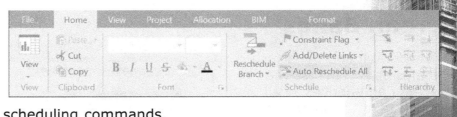

- The **Ribbon** is similar to other Microsoft products:

- **Home** – Contains the scheduling commands,

- **View** – Used to assign Filters, Views and Tables, plus other formatting commands,

- **Project** – Task Numbering, Baselines,

- **Allocation** – Commands to allocate cost and resource information,

- **BIM** – This will be displayed after purchasing a BIM license,

- **Format** – To change the Barchart (Gantt Chart) and Date Zone (Timescale) formatting,

- **Add-Ins** – This will be displayed when you load an Add-In.

Page 47

47

EASTWOOD HARRIS PTY LTD.

Customizing the Toolbars

- The toolbars will not be covered in detail in this course as they operate the same way as all other Microsoft products,

- The **Ribbon Toolbar** has Tabs along the top and Ribbon Groups, which are groups of Command Buttons, below the Ribbon Tabs,

- Significant productivity improvements may be made by:

  - Moving the **Quick Access Toolbar** below the Ribbon Toolbar,

  - Ensuring that frequently used functions are made available on the Quick Access Toolbar,

  - **Minimize the Ribbon** which hides the Ribbon Toolbar until required,

- **Note:** You will import the Eastwood Harris Powerproject Quick Access toolbar in a workshop which is available from https://www.eh.com.au/software.html.

Page 48

48

Moving columns

- To move a column place the mouse cursor in the top of the column title and it will turn into a double headed mouse,

- Then left click and drag the column to the desired position,
- The column width may be manually adjusted by clicking on the right hand side of the header and dragging left or right.

Page 49

49

Scaling the Date Zone

- Select a vertical line in the **Date Zone**,

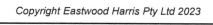

- Move the mouse in the **Date Zone** until a double headed arrow is displayed,
- Left click and drag it left or right to change the **Date Zone** scaling.

Page 50

50

EASTWOOD HARRIS PTY LTD.

Moving the Date Zone

- Left click and hold in the **Date Zone**,

- A hand icon will be displayed in the **Date Zone**,

- Drag left or right to move the **Date Zone** left or right,

- You may also use the **Scroll Bars** at the bottom of the screen to move the **Date Zone** left and right,

- There is also a **Fit All to Window** icon under the **View**, **Tab** Ribbon tab.

Copyright Eastwood Harris Pty Ltd 2023

EASTWOOD HARRIS PTY LTD.

The Project View

- The **Project View** displays project information that may be assigned to tasks and provides a method of allocating codes, resources, calendars etc.,

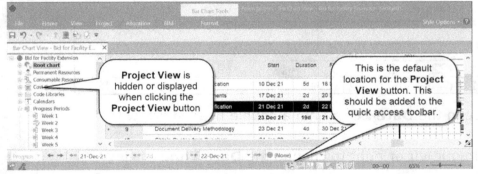

- To hide or display the **Project View** select the **Project View** icon from either the:

  - The **Status Bar** at the bottom of the screen, or

  - You should add the icon to the **Quick Access Toolbar**.

Copyright Eastwood Harris Pty Ltd 2023

Bar and Task Properties View

- Right click and select **Properties View** to hide or display a lower pane titled the **Bar & Task Propertie**s,
- There is an **Auto Hide** option on the top right hand side of the form,
- The button at the bottom displays more or less tabs in the **Bar and Task Properties** form.

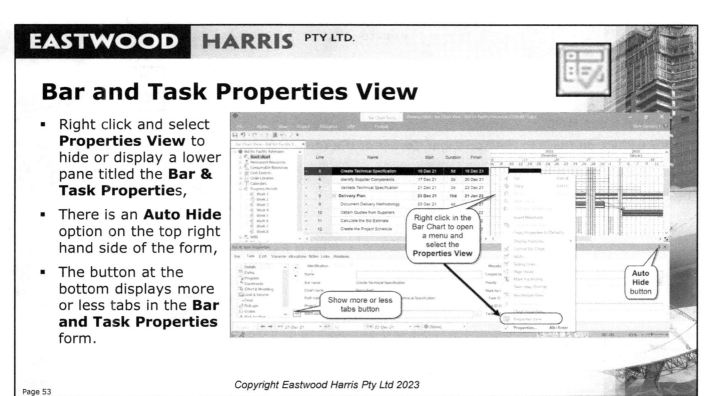

Copyright Eastwood Harris Pty Ltd 2023

Page 53

53

Bar and Task Properties Form

- The **Bar and Task Properties** form displays similar information to the **Task Properties View**:
- To open **the Bar and Task Properties** form,
- Select a task,
- Right Click and select **Properties**:

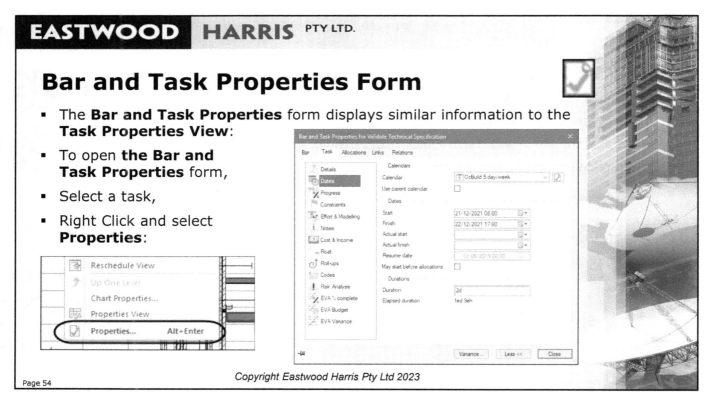

Copyright Eastwood Harris Pty Ltd 2023

Page 54

54

EASTWOOD HARRIS PTY LTD.

Help

- To Access Help:
    - Click on the ? In the Top Right Corner of the screen, or
    - Press F1:

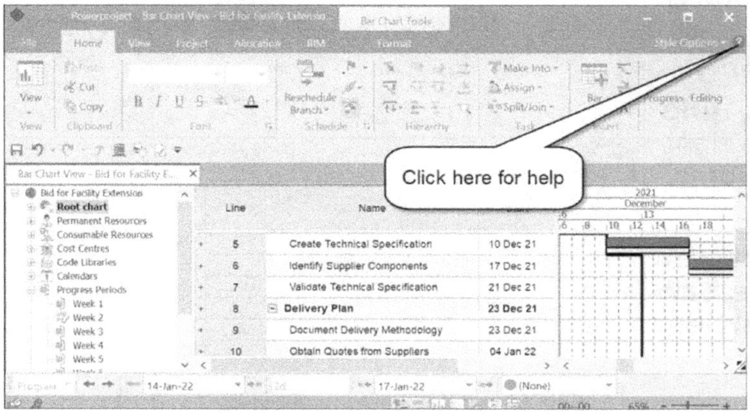

Click here for help

Line	Name	
5	Create Technical Specification	10 Dec 21
6	Identify Supplier Components	17 Dec 21
7	Validate Technical Specification	21 Dec 21
8	Delivery Plan	23 Dec 21
9	Document Delivery Methodology	23 Dec 21
10	Obtain Quotes from Suppliers	04 Jan 22

Copyright Eastwood Harris Pty Ltd 2023

Page 55

55

EASTWOOD HARRIS PTY LTD.

Workshop 2 – Navigation and Setting Your Project Options

- In this workshop you will:
    - Import the Eastwood Harris Quick Access Toolbar and
    - Practice navigating around the screen.

Copyright Eastwood Harris Pty Ltd 2023

Page 56

56

EASTWOOD HARRIS PTY LTD.

3 - CALENDARS

- **Calendars** define the working times of a project,

- The **Calendar** consists of a **Work Pattern** to which **Exceptions** may be added,

- A **Work Pattern** defines how many hours per day and days per week are worked,

- An **Exception** is work or non-work time that does not conform to the Work Pattern. E.g. holidays or overtime which are called **Non Work time** in many US software packages, or working Sundays,

- **Note:** The Powerproject Construction and Housing templates both contain Calendars which cover the most common UK working patterns,

- Customised templates should have calendars created and tailored to suit your organisation's requirements.

Page 57

57

EASTWOOD HARRIS PTY LTD.

Work Pattern

- A calendar is constructed of two components found in the **Library Explorer** and one is the **Work Patterns**,

- They are given a name,

- Each day of the week is assigned the work start and finish times,

- Assigned **Override Definitions** that are used to define summary durations in weeks, months and years,

- These topics are not covered in this course as existing Work Patterns will be used.

Page 58

58

EASTWOOD HARRIS PTY LTD.

Exceptions

- A calendar is constructed of two components that are found in the **Library Explorer** and the second one is the **Exceptions**,

- These are given a name,

- **Formatting**, allowing different work or non work to be displayed on the Gantt Chart in different colours and

- Defined as **Working time** or **Non-working** time.

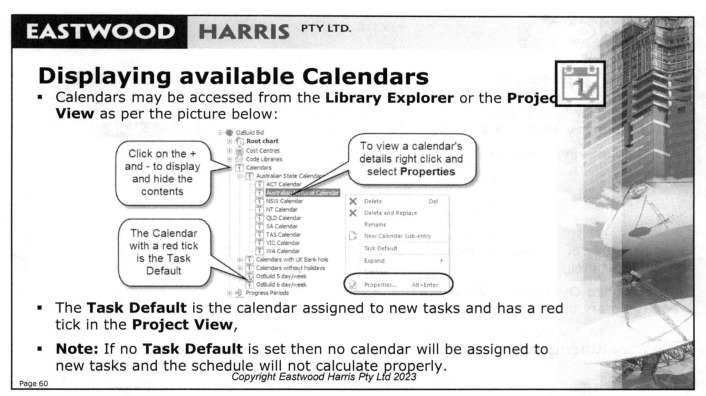

Page 59

59

EASTWOOD HARRIS PTY LTD.

Displaying available Calendars

- Calendars may be accessed from the **Library Explorer** or the **Project View** as per the picture below:

Click on the + and - to display and hide the contents

To view a calendar's details right click and select **Properties**

The Calendar with a red tick is the Task Default

- OzBuild Bid
  - Root chart
  - Cost Centres
  - Code Libraries
  - Calendars
    - Australian State Calendars
      - ACT Calendar
      - Australian National Calendar
      - NSW Calendar
      - NT Calendar
      - QLD Calendar
      - SA Calendar
      - TAS Calendar
      - VIC Calendar
      - WA Calendar
    - Calendars with UK Bank hols
    - Calendars without holidays
    - OzBuild 5 day/week
    - OzBuild 6 day/week
  - Progress Periods

X	Delete	Del
X	Delete and Replace	
	Rename	
	New Calendar Sub-entry	
	Task Default	
	Expand ►	
✓	Properties...	Alt+Enter

- The **Task Default** is the calendar assigned to new tasks and has a red tick in the **Project View**,

- **Note:** If no **Task Default** is set then no calendar will be assigned to new tasks and the schedule will not calculate properly.

Page 60

60

30

EASTWOOD HARRIS PTY LTD.

Creating New Calendars

- There are several methods of creating calendars:

- From **Library Explorer** copy an existing calendar from another project or within a project using the copy and paste commands, then rename and edit,

- Use the **New Calendar Wizard**, which may be run from either:

  - The **Library Explorer** after selecting a Calendar Node and selecting **New Calendar** or **New Calendar Sub-entry**, or

  - The **Project View** after selecting a Calendar Node and selecting **New Calendar** or **New Calendar Sub-entry**,

- You may then edit your new calendar,

- **Note:** If you have a good calendar, then it is simpler to copy and paste an existing calendar and change the **Work Pattern** and **Exceptions** and not use the **New Calendar Wizard**.

Page 61

61

EASTWOOD HARRIS PTY LTD.

Creating a new calendar using Library Explorer and the New Calendar Wizard:

- To create a new calendar open the **Library Explorer** and select the calendars folder,

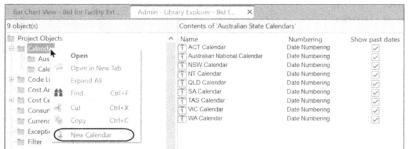

- Right click on Calendar and select **New Calendar** to run **the New Calendar Wizard**,

- A new calendar may also be created from the **Project View** by left clicking and selecting **New Calendar Sub-entry**.

Page 62

62

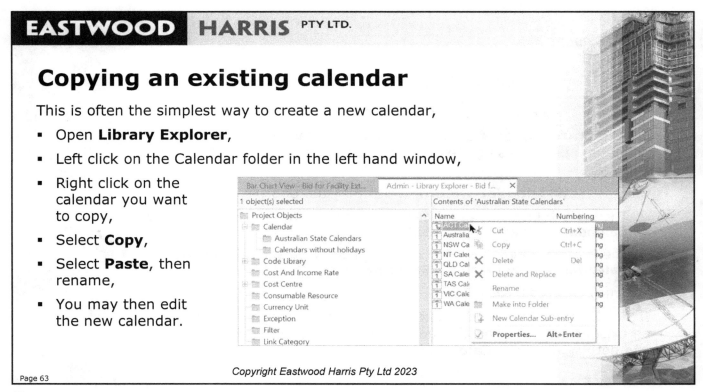

Copying an existing calendar

This is often the simplest way to create a new calendar,

- Open **Library Explorer**,
- Left click on the Calendar folder in the left hand window,
- Right click on the calendar you want to copy,
- Select **Copy**,
- Select **Paste**, then rename,
- You may then edit the new calendar.

Copyright Eastwood Harris Pty Ltd 2023

Page 63

63

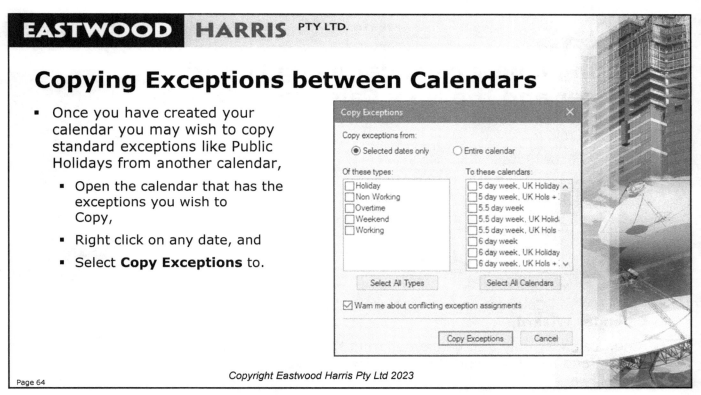

Copying Exceptions between Calendars

- Once you have created your calendar you may wish to copy standard exceptions like Public Holidays from another calendar,
  - Open the calendar that has the exceptions you wish to Copy,
  - Right click on any date, and
  - Select **Copy Exceptions** to.

Copyright Eastwood Harris Pty Ltd 2023

Page 64

64

EASTWOOD HARRIS PTY LTD.

Half Day Exception

- Each day in the Calendar has a Work Pattern assigned to it,
- An **Exception** is any day which does not follow that **Work Pattern**,
- A half tone colour, e.g. pink instead of red, would be a half day exception.

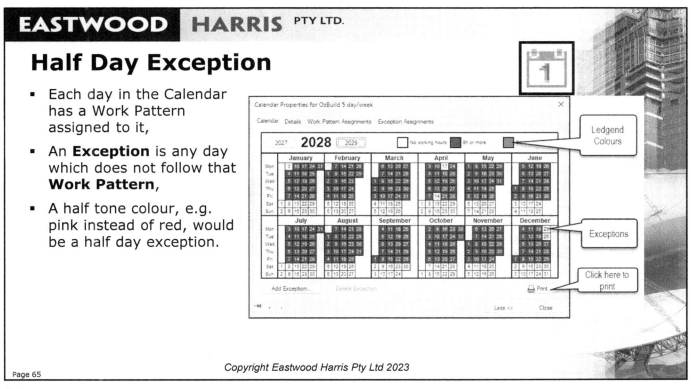

65

EASTWOOD HARRIS PTY LTD.

Viewing Working Hours

- Double click on any day to view the working hours:

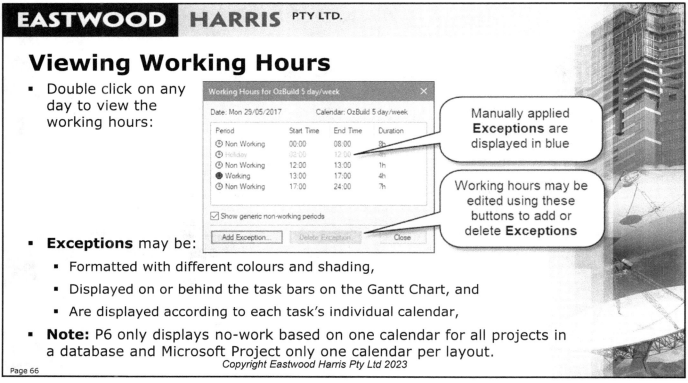

- **Exceptions** may be:
  - Formatted with different colours and shading,
  - Displayed on or behind the task bars on the Gantt Chart, and
  - Are displayed according to each task's individual calendar,
- **Note:** P6 only displays no-work based on one calendar for all projects in a database and Microsoft Project only one calendar per layout.

66

EASTWOOD HARRIS PTY LTD.

Adding Calendar Exceptions

- To change working days into holiday or weekends into working days in your calendar:

- Left click on one or more date(s), these will now be highlighted in blue,

- Right Click and select the **Assign Exception**,

- Select the type of exception, e.g. Holiday,

- Then either:

  - Enter **Start and end times**, or

  - Tick the boxes to apply the exception **From work pattern periods** for both **morning** and **afternoon**, **Note:** This is the recommended method, as the format of calendar non-work time and work time is the same, or

  - Select 24 hour,

  - **Exceptions** may also be edited in the **Exception Assignments** tab.

EASTWOOD HARRIS PTY LTD.

Deleting Calendar Exceptions

- Ctrl + Left click to select date(s),

- Click on the **Delete all exception assignments** button to delete both Morning and Afternoon Exceptions when applied,

- Click **Yes** when prompted, this is not prompted in later versions:

EASTWOOD HARRIS PTY LTD.

Task Default Calendar...

- The **Task Default** calendar is assigned to all new tasks,

- Changing the **Task Default** calendar will not change the calendar assigned to any existing tasks, only new tasks,

- If using the "Powerproject Construction Template" you will see that there are a number of calendars to cover 5, 6 or 7 working day calendars with and without public holidays, which are based on the UK practices,

- You may copy and paste in **Library Explorer** to make copy an existing calendar:

  - To create new calendar in a project and edit it to manage work on different working times, or

  - Copy a calendar from one project to another,

- You may create your own new calendar using the **New Calendar Wizard**.

Page 69   *Copyright Eastwood Harris Pty Ltd 2023*

69

EASTWOOD HARRIS PTY LTD.

Task Default Calendar

- The **Task Default** calendar is:

  - The one with the red tick in the **Project View**, and

  - Is assigned to new tasks when they are created,

- To change the default Calendar:

  - Open the **Project View** and Navigate to your chosen Calendar,

  - Right Click and select Task Default,

  - **Note:** This is now the calendar that will be assigned to new tasks,

  - The Calendar Settings form is then displayed which gives you some options that will be explained on the next slide.

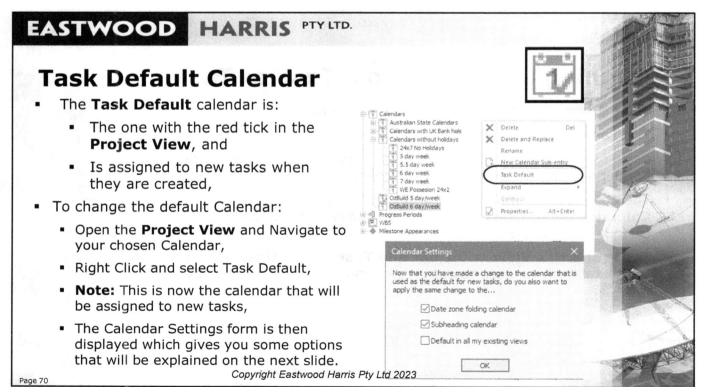

Page 70   *Copyright Eastwood Harris Pty Ltd 2023*

70

EASTWOOD HARRIS PTY LTD.

Calendar Settings form

- **Date zone folding** calendar is the calendar used to hide non work time in the Gantt chart, covered in Formatting the Display section,

- Subheading calendar is explained in the picture below:

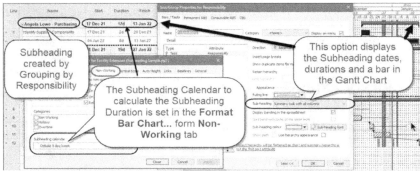

- Default in all views will assign the options selected above to all the other user views, but not project views.

Page 71

71

EASTWOOD HARRIS PTY LTD.

Assigning a Calendar to a Task or Tasks

- The methods of assigning calendars to tasks are:

- The **Task Default** calendar is assigned when a task is created,

- One or more selected task/s may have their calendar changed by dragging a new calendar from the **Project View**,

- The **Calendar** column may be displayed or a table created with the **Calendar** column, then copy and paste may be used to assign a calendar to multiple tasks,

- The **Properties View** or the **Bar and Task Properties** form **Task, Dates** tab may be used to assign a calendar to a single task at a time.

Page 72

72

EASTWOOD HARRIS PTY LTD.

Assigning a Calendar to a task

- Calendars may be assigned to a single task in the **Bar and Task Properties** form or view, **Task**, **Dates** tab,

Bar & Task Properties							⤢ ×
Bar Task EVA Variance Allocations Notes Links Relations							
Details		Dates					
Dates		Start	4/01/2022 08:00		Calendar	OzBuild 5 day/week	
Progress		Finish	13/01/2022 17:00				

- Another way is to open the **Project View**,

- Then left click on the desired calendar, and drag the calendar on to one of the selected task bars:

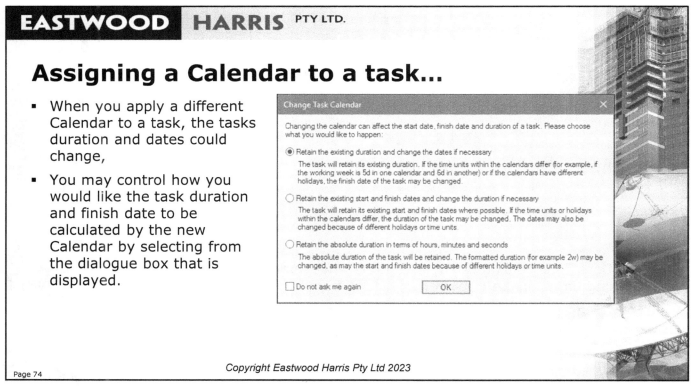

- **Note:** Select the Gantt Chart bars or the Line Number before dragging when assigning to multiple tasks.

Page 73

Copyright Eastwood Harris Pty Ltd 2023

73

EASTWOOD HARRIS PTY LTD.

Assigning a Calendar to a task...

- When you apply a different Calendar to a task, the tasks duration and dates could change,

- You may control how you would like the task duration and finish date to be calculated by the new Calendar by selecting from the dialogue box that is displayed.

Change Task Calendar   ✕

Changing the calendar can affect the start date, finish date and duration of a task. Please choose what you would like to happen:

⦿ Retain the existing duration and change the dates if necessary

The task will retain its existing duration. If the time units within the calendars differ (for example, if the working week is 5d in one calendar and 6d in another) or if the calendars have different holidays, the finish date of the task may be changed.

◯ Retain the existing start and finish dates and change the duration if necessary

The task will retain its existing start and finish dates where possible. If the time units or holidays within the calendars differ, the duration of the task may be changed. The dates may also be changed because of different holidays or time units.

◯ Retain the absolute duration in terms of hours, minutes and seconds

The absolute duration of the task will be retained. The formatted duration (for example 2w) may be changed, as may the start and finish dates because of different holidays or time units.

☐ Do not ask me again   OK

Page 74

Copyright Eastwood Harris Pty Ltd 2023

74

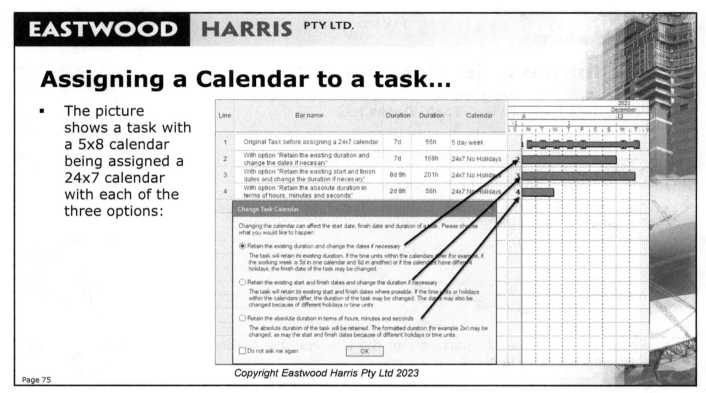

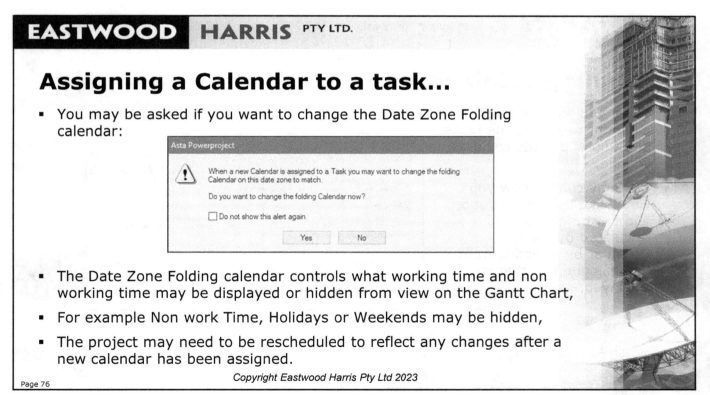

EASTWOOD HARRIS PTY LTD.

Assigning a Calendar to multiple tasks

- Select the tasks to be assigned a new calendar by either:
  - Clicking on the row number to select the whole line, or
  - Selecting the bars in the Gantt Chart,
  - **Note:** the Gantt Charts bars must be highlighted,
- Open the **Project View**,
- Click the + next to Calendars to reveal the available Calendars,
- Left click on the desired calendar, hold the mouse button down and drag the Calendar on to a task and let go of the mouse button,
- Again you will be given choices as to how you would like to change your tasks as a result of the new Calendar.

Page 77

77

EASTWOOD HARRIS PTY LTD.

Assigning a Calendar to the whole Project

- Select Ctrl A to select all activities,
- Open the **Project View**,
- Click the + next to Calendars to reveal the available Calendars,
- Left click on the desired calendar, hold the mouse button down and drag the Calendar on to a task and let go of the mouse button,
- Again you will be given choices as to how you would like to change your tasks as a result of the new Calendar.

Page 78

78

EASTWOOD HARRIS PTY LTD.

Formatting Exceptions Display on the Gantt Chart

- The display of Exception's Nonwork and Working time and colours is determined by the Format Bar Chart, Non-Working tab:

  - Non-working display necks the bars and must be unchecked to Draw Non-working shading On tasks,

  - Draw Non-working shading On tasks shades the Chart or Tasks,

  - Colours and patterns are set in the Library Explorer, Exception tab,

  - Categories selects what is shaded with the options above.

Format Bar Chart (Bar Chart View - OzBuild Workshop 01 (OzBuild Workshop 01.pp) \Summary Task)

Tasks Schedule Allocations Progress **Non-Working** Vertical Scale Auto Height Links Baselines General

Non-working display
- [ ] On tasks
- [ ] On allocations

Draw non-working shading
- [x] On chart
- [x] On tasks
- [x] On allocations
- [x] Remove outline

Standard work shading
- [ ] On chart
  - [x] Default Standard Work

Categories
- [ ] Non Working
- [x] Holiday
- [ ] Overtime
- [ ] Weekend

Subheading calendar
5 day week

Necking
Neck summary tasks to show where no tasks

Close   Cancel   Apply

Copyright Eastwood Harris Pty Ltd 2023

79

EASTWOOD HARRIS PTY LTD.

Workshop 3 - Maintaining the Calendars

- We will create and edit two calendars for your project,
- You will create:

  - A 5 day per week calendar with some holidays by copying an exiting calendar and

  - A 6 day per week calendar by copying the 5 day per week calendar and edit it to create a new calendar with the same holidays.

Copyright Eastwood Harris Pty Ltd 2023

80

EASTWOOD HARRIS PTY LTD.

4 - TASKS AND MILESTONES

In this module we will look at:

- Creating tasks
- Moving and editing tasks
- Creating milestones.

Page 81

81

EASTWOOD HARRIS PTY LTD.

Creating tasks

- A task may be created by either:
    - Typing a name and duration into the column on the Spreadsheet, or
    - By using the cursor to draw onto the Bar Chart and then entering a name on the Spreadsheet,
- Once created, any task attribute may be edited using either the Spreadsheet or using the mouse on the task bar,
- Tasks may be added:
    - At the bottom of the list of tasks, or
    - By inserting a new task by right clicking and selecting Insert Bar, which inserts a task above the selected task, or
    - By inserting a new task by right clicking and selecting Insert Bar Below.

Page 82

82

EASTWOOD HARRIS PTY LTD.

To Create tasks in the Spreadsheet

- Select the duration column for the first blank task,
- Enter the duration,
- Press Enter,
- A task is displayed on the Bar Chart,
- Enter the Name.

Line	Name	Start	Duration	Finish	May
					20	27
					135	136	137
1	First Task Name	20/05/19	3d	22/05/19	1

Page 83

83

EASTWOOD HARRIS PTY LTD.

To create tasks on the Bar Chart

- Click the mouse on the Bar Chart on a line for the next task, the cursor will now be a cross,
- Left click and drag the mouse to the right,

Line	Name	Start	Duration	Finish	May
					20	27
					Start	23/05/19	137
1	First Task Name	20/05/19	3d	22/05/19	Finish	27/05/19
					Duration	3d

- The pop up box displays the task duration,
- The task name may be typed in before or after the task is created in the Gantt Chart.

Page 84

84

EASTWOOD HARRIS PTY LTD.

Sorting and the Task Order

- As tasks are added they adopt the Natural Order,

- When a user double clicks on a task column header the tasks are sorted in ascending and then descending in the order of the column values,

- This often happens by accident and to bring the tasks back to the Natural Order you should select **View**, **View data**, **Natural Order**:

This schedule was put out of order by right clicking on the Start heading and selecting **Sort Descending** or by double clicking on the heading.

85

EASTWOOD HARRIS PTY LTD.

Moving and editing tasks

- Tasks may be moved and edited using either the mouse or the Object Edit Toolbar,

- Edit the Task Duration by editing the start or end date,

- Edit the Task Dates by simply moving the task to another position on the Gantt Chart,

- If your Reschedule Options is set to Auto reschedule then the task may just move back to the original start date location.

86

EASTWOOD HARRIS PTY LTD.

Using the mouse to adjust durations and dates:

- Tasks may be edited using either the mouse by placing the mouse at either end of the task or in the middle:

  - Placed in the middle adjusts the position of the task,

  - Placed at the start adjusts the Start Date, and changes the duration,

  - Placed at the end adjusts the End Date, and changes the duration,

- **Note:** When the Reschedule Options are set to Move to ASAP/ALAP and Auto reschedule then then this will schedule tasks and these commands will only adjust the durations of the tasks.

EASTWOOD HARRIS PTY LTD.

Editing the Object Edit Toolbar

- The option to hide the Object Edit toolbar was removed in Version 14,
- Right click on the Object Edit Toolbar and select Customize to edit it:

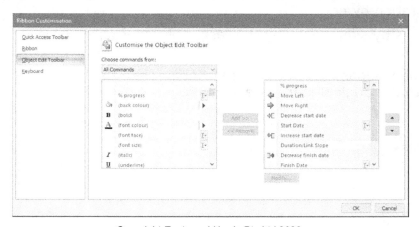

EASTWOOD HARRIS PTY LTD.

The Object Edit Toolbar:

- Select a task on the Gantt Chart using the ◄▭► cursor,
- The Object Edit toolbar is now active at the bottom of the screen:

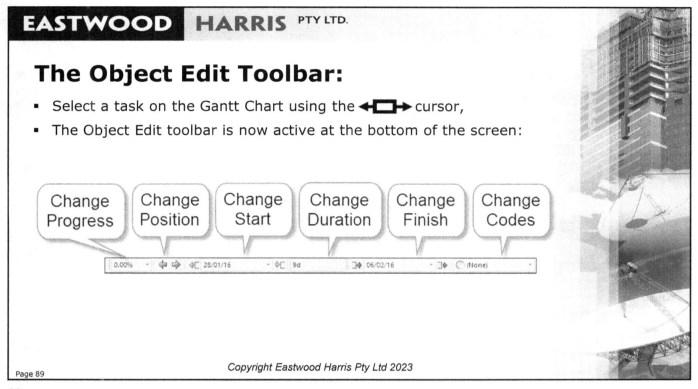

EASTWOOD HARRIS PTY LTD.

Moving bars vertically

- Moving bars vertically allows you to change the order of tasks within the project,
- Left click on the line number for the task you want to move. This selects the entire bar of information on both the Spreadsheet data and task on the Bar Chart,

- Place the cursor over the task bar until the cursor ◄▭► is displayed shown in the picture above,
- Click and drag the bar to the new line above,
- **Note:** An applied View with a sort order may prevent this action.

Inserting bars

- To insert a new bar above a task:
    - Left click on the line number below where you want to insert your new line, Right click and select Insert Bar,

Line	Name	Duration	Start	Finish	Total float	Free float
1	Approval to Bid		06 Dec 21	06 Dec 21	8d	8d
2	Determine Installation Requirements	4d	06 Dec 21	09 Dec 21	4d	4d
3		5d	06 Dec 21	10 Dec 21	3d	3d
4		2d	06 Dec 21	07 Dec 21	6d	6d
5		2d	06 Dec 21	07 Dec 21	6d	6d
6		4d	06 Dec 21	09 Dec 21	4d	4d
7		8d	06 Dec 21	15 Dec 21	0d	0d
8		3d	06 Dec 21	08 Dec 21	6d	6d

Context menu:
- Cut — Ctrl+X
- Copy — Ctrl+C
- Paste — Ctrl+V
- Paste Values
- Paste and Retain Links
- Insert Bar — Ins
- Insert Bar Below
- Delete — Del

- To insert a new bar below a task:
    - Left click on the line number below where you want to insert your new line, Right click and select Insert Bar Below.

Understanding Milestones

- There are 2 types of Powerproject milestones, Start and Finish,

- Powerproject milestones calculate in a similar way to P6 milestones but display both Start and Finish Dates. Microsoft Project Milestones always calculate as a Powerproject Finish Milestone:
    - A Start Milestone will appear at the start of the next available work period, usually at the same time as the successor,
    - A Finish Milestone will appear at the end of the current work period, usually at the same time as the predecessor,

- E.g. if a predecessor task is completed on Friday afternoon,
    - A successor Finish Milestone will appear at the end of Friday afternoon,
    - A successor Start Milestone will appear on Monday morning,

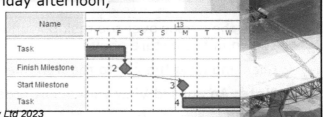

- A Start Milestone is created by default.

EASTWOOD HARRIS PTY LTD.

Creating a Start Milestone

- To create a Start Milestone either,
    - Type in the Milestone name in a blank line and
    - Enter 0 in the duration column,

Line	Name	Duration	Start	Finish	Total float	Free float	Nov 29	December 6	13
							-1	1	2
1	Approval to Bid		06 Dec 21	06 Dec 21	8d	8d	1		
2	Determine Installation Requirements	4d	06 Dec 21	09 Dec 21	4d	4d	2		
3	Create Technical Specification	5d	06 Dec 21	10 Dec 21	3d	3d	3		

- Or, go to the first blank line at the bottom of the screen in the Gantt Chart,
    - Right click and select Insert Milestone and
    - Type in the Milestone name:
- **Note:** The 0 Duration may not be displayed when the default is to display zeros as blank in the Table Definition Properties form.

EASTWOOD HARRIS PTY LTD.

To change a Start Milestone into a Finish Milestone:

- Right click on the Milestone icon in the Gantt Chart and select Make into – Finish Milestone:

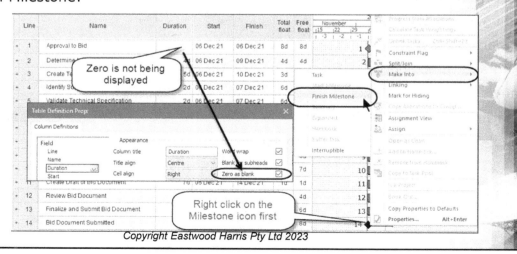

EASTWOOD HARRIS PTY LTD.

Workshop 4 - Adding Tasks

- In this workshop you will add the project tasks,

- It is simpler to teach Powerproject by showing how you to enter the tasks first and then creating the summary tasks to represent the WBS Nodes which also called Products or Deliverables,

- Once a user understands the processes then the tasks and summary tasks may be entered in any order.

Page 95

95

EASTWOOD HARRIS PTY LTD.

5 - SUMMARY TASKS

This module will cover the following topics:

- Understanding Summary Tasks,

- Creating Summary tasks,

- Summarising tasks,

- Adding and removing tasks from Summary Tasks,

- Removing Summary Tasks,

- Formatting Summary Tasks and

- Navigating a program using the Project View and Summary Tasks.

Page 96

96

EASTWOOD HARRIS PTY LTD.

Understanding Summary Tasks

- Summary Tasks are used to summarize and group tasks under a hierarchy of Parent or Summary Tasks,

- They are used to present different views of your project during planning, scheduling and updating,

- These headings are normally based on your project WBS,

- Summary Tasks may be used to represent one or more of the following:

  - Work Breakdown Structure

  - The project phases and stages

  - Areas, floor or physical locations

  - Trades of disciplines

  - Systems and sub-systems

- **Note:** Summary Tasks calculate in a similar way to Microsoft Project Summary Tasks and P6 WBS activities.

Page 97

97

EASTWOOD HARRIS PTY LTD.

Creating a summary task

- Highlight the bars you wish to summarise,

- Click the **Summarise** button on the **Home** toolbar, **Hierarchy** group:

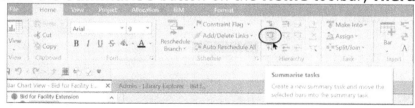

- This will create a Summary Task above the selected tasks without a Name,

- Enter the summary task name:

Line	Name	Duration	Start	Finish	Total float	Free float	December 2021
1	⊟ Technical Specification	5d	06 Dec 21	10 Dec 21	3d	3d	
2	Approval to Bid		06 Dec 21	06 Dec 21	8d	8d	
3	Determine Installation Requirements	4d	06 Dec 21	09 Dec 21	4d	4d	
4	Create Technical Specification	5d	06 Dec 21	10 Dec 21	3d	3d	
5	Identify Supplier Components	2d	06 Dec 21	07 Dec 21	6d	6d	

Page 98

98

Rolling up and opening summary tasks

- Highlight the Summary Task bar in the Gantt Chart so the ◀▭▶ pointer is displayed and double click,

- Double click again to display the tasks,

- The **Show To Level button** may also be used to summarise tasks to Levels:

- Clicking on the + and – to the left of the Task Name, as with Microsoft Project,

- **Note:** The **Show To Level button** function will only operate to Level 1 and All Levels when the tasks are grouped by codes.

Copyright Eastwood Harris Pty Ltd 2023

Page 99

99

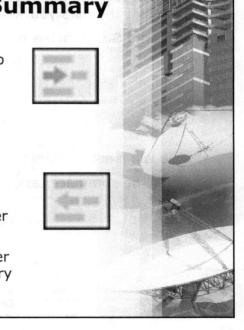

Adding & Removing Tasks from Summary Task

- Select the task or tasks by clicking on the line number to select the bar(s),

- To add a task to a Summary Task click on the Indent button on the Home toolbar, Hierarchy group:

- Bars are added to the summary that is above the selected task or tasks,

- To remove a task from a Summary Task click on the Outdent button on the Home toolbar, Hierarchy group, which will outdent the task or tasks so they are no longer under the summary task,

- **Note:** Unlike Microsoft Project, outdenting all tasks under a Summary Task in Powerproject will delete the Summary Task.

Copyright Eastwood Harris Pty Ltd 2023

Page 100

100

Deleting Summary Tasks

To delete a Summary Task either:

- Select all the tasks under a Summary Task,

- Click the Outdent button from the **Home** toolbar, **Hierarchy** group,

- The Summary Task will be deleted after the last Task has been Outdented,

Or:

- Delete the Summary Task which will also delete all of the Detailed Tasks underneath,

Note: Deleting all Detailed Tasks under a Summary Task will not delete a Summary Task and you will end up with a Summary Task with no Detailed Tasks under it.

Page 101

101

Summary Bar Background Formatting

- The background colour and spreadsheet cell font and colour for Summary Tasks bars may be formatted in the **Project View**,

- The formatting must be created by selecting a node in the **Project View**, right clicking and selecting **Appearance...**

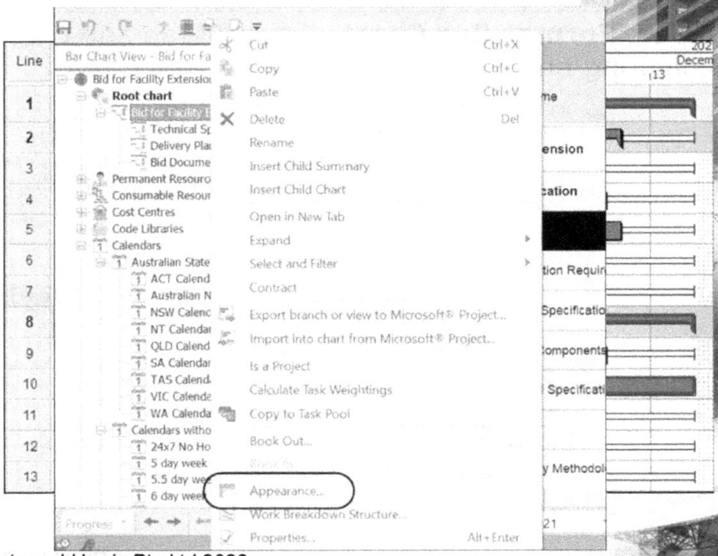

Page 102

102

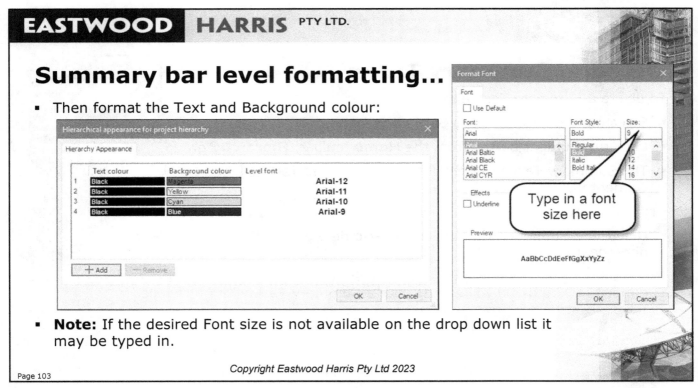

Copyright Eastwood Harris Pty Ltd 2023

Page 103

103

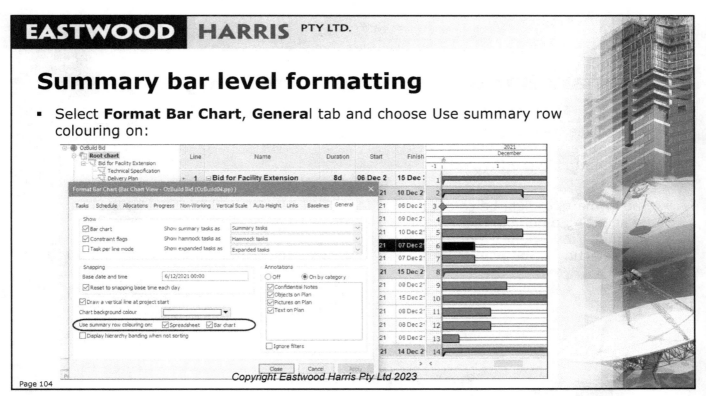

Copyright Eastwood Harris Pty Ltd 2023

Page 104

104

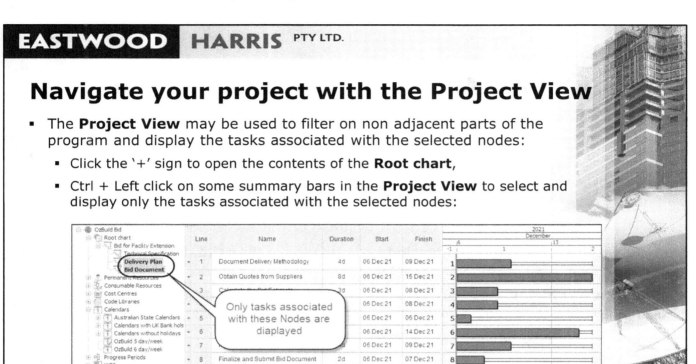

Navigate your project with the Project View

- The **Project View** may be used to filter on non adjacent parts of the program and display the tasks associated with the selected nodes:

  - Click the '+' sign to open the contents of the **Root chart**,

  - Ctrl + Left click on some summary bars in the **Project View** to select and display only the tasks associated with the selected nodes:

Workshop 5 - Entering Summary Tasks

In this workshop you will create some Summary Tasks,

- A Summary Task at Level 1 for Phase entitled **Bid for Facility Extension** and

- A Summary at Level 2 for each of the three Products the project is delivering:

  - **Technical Specification**

  - **Delivery Plan**

  - **Bid Document**

EASTWOOD HARRIS PTY LTD.

6 - LINKING TASKS TO CREATE A CRITICAL PATH SCHEDULE

- This module will cover how to link tasks to create a critical path program,

- The predecessor is the task at the start of the link and the successor is the task at the end of the link,

- The predecessor controls the start or finish of the successor,

- When there are multiple links between two tasks then the driving predecessor/s control/s the start or finish of the successor,

- **Link Categories** may be assigned to links so they may formatted or made inactive, in turn allowing multiple logic options in one program,

- **Links** may also be assigned **Notes**.

Copyright Eastwood Harris Pty Ltd 2023

Page 107

107

EASTWOOD HARRIS PTY LTD.

Understanding Leads and Lags in Powerproject

- Microsoft Project and Primavera P6 calculate the lead or lag on the link, thus the link is assigned the lead or lag, but

- Powerproject calculates the leads and lags on the predecessor and/or successor tasks,

- A Powerproject lead or lag is specified from the start or finish of the predecessor or successor in duration or percent of the task duration, thus allowing:

  - An unlimited number of links between tasks,

  - The lag calendar to be either the predecessor's or successor's or both and

  - Partial Critical Paths calculated through tasks.

Copyright Eastwood Harris Pty Ltd 2023

Page 108

108

EASTWOOD HARRIS PTY LTD.

Preparing to Link Tasks using the Root Chart

- Often it is better to reduce the number of tasks in view by selecting the appropriate nodes in the **Root chart**,

- This function may only be used when tasks are grouped under Summary Tasks, but may not be used when tasks are grouped by codes or other attributes,

- The picture below shows only the tasks under the two selected Summary tasks:

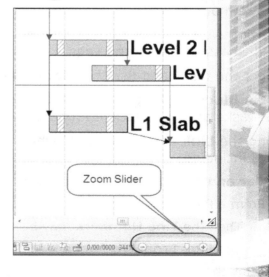

109

EASTWOOD HARRIS PTY LTD.

Preparing to Link Tasks using Zoom Slider

- To make it simpler to assign Link consider using the **Zoom Slider** before adding Links to enlarge the task bars,

- Unlike Microsoft Project this function does not mess up your **Date Zone** formatting.

Level 2 |

Lev

L1 Slab

Zoom Slider

110

55

EASTWOOD HARRIS PTY LTD.

Link types

- There are 4 types of links as in other software:

  - **Finish to Start**, or often called a **Normal** link,

  - **Start to Start**

  - **Finish to Finish**

  - **Start to Finish**, which is illogical as the successor is before the predecessor,

- The predecessor controls the start or finish of the successor,

- The direction of the arrow goes from the predecessor to successor and

- Links may also be drawn starting and ending anywhere along the length of a predecessor or successor which creates a **Lead** or **Lag**.

Page 111

111

EASTWOOD HARRIS PTY LTD.

Creating Links

There are many ways to create links:

- Drawing with the mouse, which is the most natural method and may be used to assign Leads and Lags,

- Select the tasks and use the **Block Linking** function,

- **Note: Block Linking** only links from top to bottom and not in the order that tasks are selected like Primavera P6 and Microsoft Project,

- Using the **Link From/To** form, which may be opened in a number of ways including:

  - **Bar and Task Properties** form or view,

  - From a Predecessor or Successor column,

    - Then the **Line Numbers** may be typed in or

    - The **Link From/To** form opened,

  - Gant chart menu.

Page 112

112

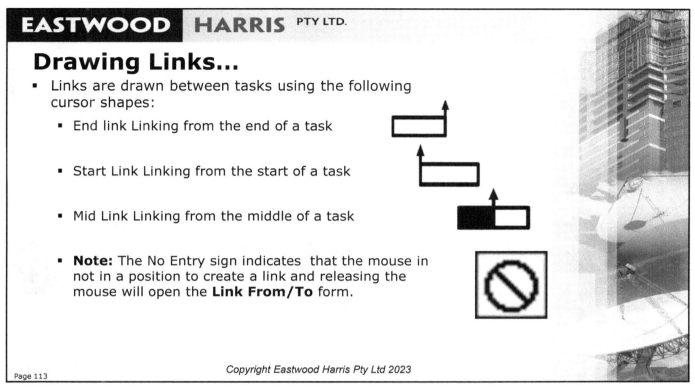

EASTWOOD HARRIS PTY LTD.

Drawing Links...

- Links are drawn between tasks using the following cursor shapes:

  - End link Linking from the end of a task

  - Start Link Linking from the start of a task

  - Mid Link Linking from the middle of a task

  - **Note:** The No Entry sign indicates that the mouse in not in a position to create a link and releasing the mouse will open the **Link From/To** form.

Page 113

113

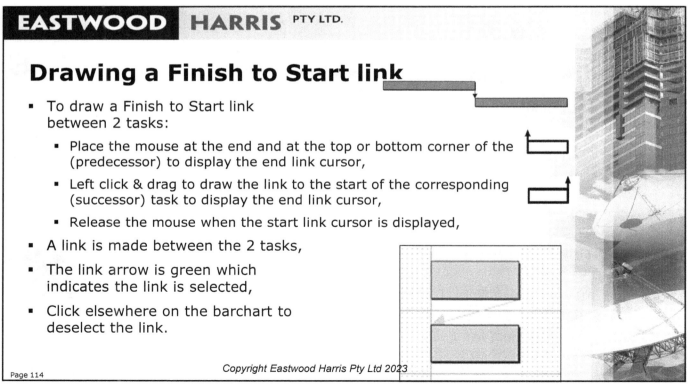

EASTWOOD HARRIS PTY LTD.

Drawing a Finish to Start link

- To draw a Finish to Start link between 2 tasks:

  - Place the mouse at the end and at the top or bottom corner of the (predecessor) to display the end link cursor,

  - Left click & drag to draw the link to the start of the corresponding (successor) task to display the end link cursor,

  - Release the mouse when the start link cursor is displayed,

- A link is made between the 2 tasks,

- The link arrow is green which indicates the link is selected,

- Click elsewhere on the barchart to deselect the link.

Page 114

114

Drawing other links without lag

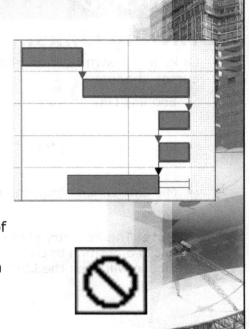

- To draw:
    - Start to Start links, or
    - Finish to Finish links, or
    - Start to Finish links,
- Place the mouse at the start or end and at the top or bottom corner of the first (predecessor) and displaying the start or end link cursor,
- Left click & drag to draw the link to the start or finish of the corresponding (successor) task,
- Dragging into a blank area will display a **No Entry** sign and releasing the mouse will open the **Link From/To** form and link information may be manually entered.

Copyright Eastwood Harris Pty Ltd 2023

Page 115

115

Drawing Mid Links...

- Leads are called Negative Lags in products such as Microsoft Project and P6,
- This document will use the term Leads,
- In Powerproject a Lead or Lag is assigned to the task and not the link,
- A predecessor and a successor may both be assigned a Lead or Lag,
- A **Mid Link** is created when either the predecessor or successor or both have a Lead or Lag,
- A link may be drawn from the middle of the predecessor and/or to middle of a successor to create a **Mid Link**,
- Thus in Powerproject the Lead or Lag is assigned to the tasks and not on the Link as in P6 or Microsoft Project.

Copyright Eastwood Harris Pty Ltd 2023

Page 116

116

EASTWOOD **HARRIS** PTY LTD.

Drawing a Mid Link

To draw a **Mid Link**:

- Place the cursor in the middle of the task so that the **Mid Link** cursor is displayed,

- A pop up box will indicate where during the task you are linking from, i.e. the Lead or Lag that you are assigning,

  - A positive value is a Lag from the start,

  - A negative value is a Lead from the end,

- Left click at the desired position and drag the pointer to the desired position on the successor task,

- Release the mouse when the corresponding link cursor is displayed,

- Double Click on the link to open the **Link Properties** form to review the link details.

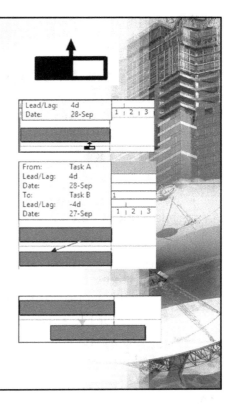

Page 117

117

EASTWOOD **HARRIS** PTY LTD.

Drawing Mid Links with a Predecessor Lag

- When a predecessor **Mid Link** is drawn there are two options for the position of the predecessor **Mid Link**, it may be calculated from:

  - A distance from the start of the predecessor, or

  - A distance from the predecessor's nearest end point,

- When the mouse is placed over the middle of a predecessor **Mid Link** is calculated from the:

  - Start of the predecessor task plus a Lag,

- When the mouse is placed over the middle of a predecessor and the **Crtl** key is pressed then the **Mid Link** is calculated from the nearest end point and is be calculated either from the:

  - Start of the predecessor task plus a Lag, or

  - A Lead (Negative Lag) from the end of the predecessor task, as per the lower picture.

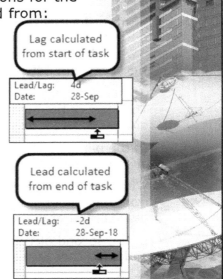

Page 118

118

EASTWOOD HARRIS PTY LTD.

Drawing Mid Links with a Successor Lag

- There are two options for the position of the successor **Mid Link** when a **Mid Link** is drawn to a successor, it may be calculated from:
  - A distance from the end of the successor, or
  - A distance from the successor's nearest end point,
- When the mouse is drawn to the middle of a successor the Mid Link is calculated by the:
  - Finish of the successor less a Lead,
- When the mouse is drawn to the middle of a successor and the Crtl key is pressed then the **Mid Link** is calculated from the nearest end from the:
  - Finish of the successor less a Lead, or
  - Start of the successor task plus a Lag, see the second picture.

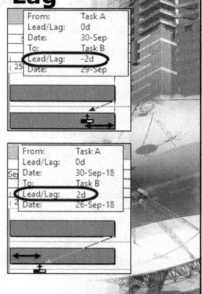

Copyright Eastwood Harris Pty Ltd 2023

Page 119

119

EASTWOOD HARRIS PTY LTD.

Drawing Mid Links with Predecessor and Successor Lead or Lag

- When a **Mid Link** is drawn from the middle of a predecessor to the middle of a successor, there are two options for the calculation of the position of the successor **Mid Link**, it may be calculated from:
  - The start of the predecessor plus a Lag to the end of the successor less a Lead,
  - In the picture the predecessor Lag is 6d and successor Lead is -6d, or
  - When the **Ctrl** key is held down then it is drawn from nearest end of the predecessor task to the nearest end of the successor task,
  - In the second picture the predecessor Lead is -2d and successor Lag is 2d.

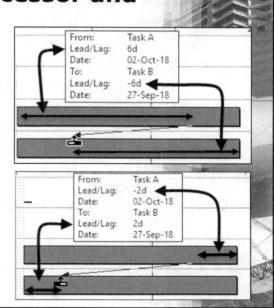

Copyright Eastwood Harris Pty Ltd 2023

Page 120

120

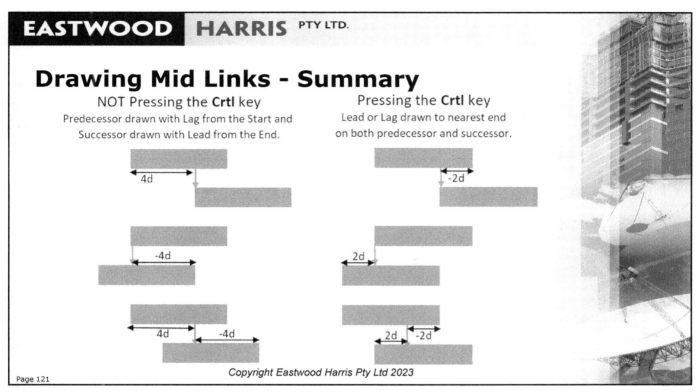

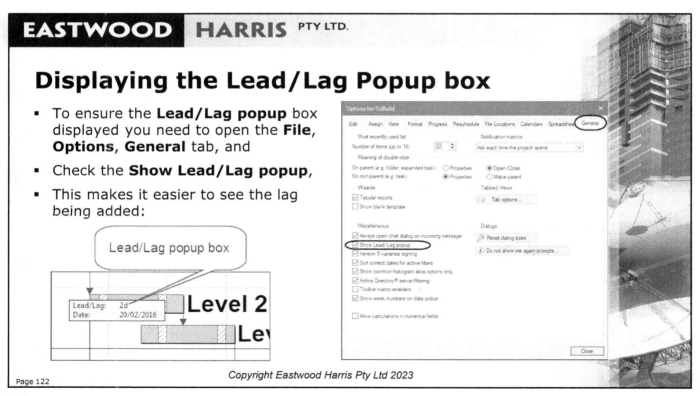

Drawing links with a FS + Lag...

- To create a link with a:
  - Finish to Start with a Lag on the predecessor, or
  - Finish to Finish with a Lag on the predecessor, or
  - Joining to any point on the successor,
- Place the cursor at the predecessor task bottom right hand corner, when link icon appears, press and hold the **Shift** key,
- Left click and hold the left mouse key down,
- Keep holding the right mouse button and drag the cursor right horizontally,

Continues on next slide...

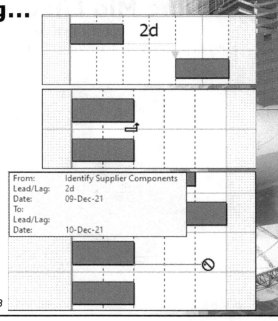

Page 123

123

Drawing links with a FS + Lag

- Once you have reached the required lag RELEASE THE SHIFT KEY but keep hold of your mouse button,

- Drag to the successor and select the point at which you wish to link too on the successor and release the mouse,

- **Note:** This is often considered bad practice as it represents a missing task, but this demonstrates how the software operates.

Page 124

124

EASTWOOD HARRIS PTY LTD.

How Mid Links are Calculated

- In many other software packages like Microsoft Project and Primavera P6:
  - The lead or lag is calculated on the link and is assigned a calendar for all tasks in one project,
  - In Microsoft Project the successor calendar is used, and
  - In Primavera P6 there is a choice of 4 calendars, predecessor, successor, 24 hour or Project Default,
- Powerproject has more flexibility and a lead or lag:
  - May be put on either or both the predecessor or successor tasks,
  - A lead or lag may be placed at a duration from the start point or end point of both the predecessor and successor,
  - The lead or lag is calculated on the respective task calendar,
  - Multiple Mid Links are allowed between two tasks,
  - Partial Critical paths may be calculated for tasks with more than one link between them.

Page 125   *Copyright Eastwood Harris Pty Ltd 2023*

125

EASTWOOD HARRIS PTY LTD.

Linking tasks from the Gantt Chart Right click menu

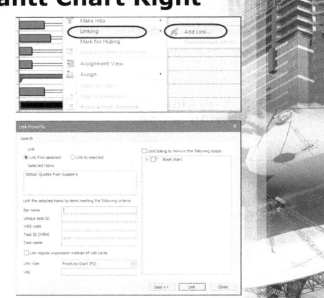

- To link multiple tasks from the Gantt Chart right click menu or clicking on a tool bar **Add Link** icon:
  - Select the task or tasks to be linked,
  - Right click in the Gantt Chart,
  - Select **Linking**, **Add Link...**, or
  - Click on the **Add Link** tool bar icon,
  - The **Link From/To** form will be displayed,
  - Click on **More>>** to show more fields,
  - A this point there are some options explained on the next slide.

Page 126   *Copyright Eastwood Harris Pty Ltd 2023*

126

EASTWOOD HARRIS PTY LTD.

Linking tasks from the Gantt Chart left click menu

One option is:

- Select either the **Link to selected** or **Link from selected** option,

- Complete the rest of the criteria by typing in the boxes underneath Link the selected items meeting the following criteria,

- **Note:** there is no lookup in these fields, but there is a lookup in the option on the next slide,

- When you click on **Link** there is no confirmation and it is difficult to see the result.

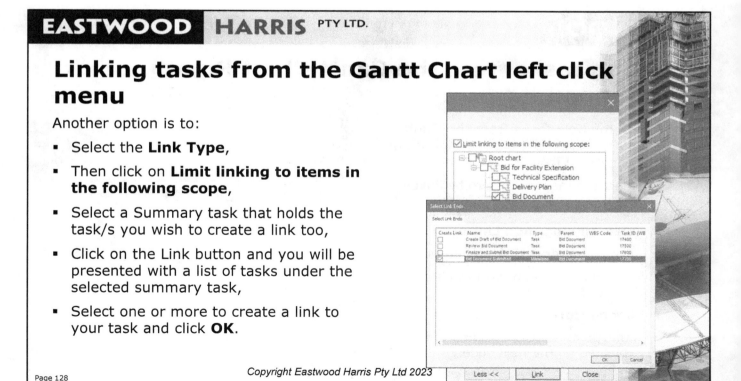

Page 127

127

EASTWOOD HARRIS PTY LTD.

Linking tasks from the Gantt Chart left click menu

Another option is to:

- Select the **Link Type**,

- Then click on **Limit linking to items in the following scope**,

- Select a Summary task that holds the task/s you wish to create a link too,

- Click on the Link button and you will be presented with a list of tasks under the selected summary task,

- Select one or more to create a link to your task and click **OK**.

Page 128

128

EASTWOOD HARRIS PTY LTD.

Dragging into a blank area to open the Link From/To form

- The **Link From/To** form may be displayed when you draw a link into a blank area of the Bar Chart and proceed as outlined in earlier slides:

Link From/To form

- Search
- Link
  - ⦿ Link from selected   ○ Link to selected
  - Selected Items
    - Create Technical Specification
- ☐ Limit linking to items in the following scope:
  - ⊞ ☐ Root chart
- Link the selected items to items meeting the following criteria:
  - Bar name
  - Unique task ID
  - WBS code
  - Task ID (WBN)
  - Task name
- ☐ Use regular expression instead of wild cards
- Link type   Finish-to-Start (FS)
- Lag
- Less <<   Link   Close

129

EASTWOOD HARRIS PTY LTD.

Linking

- Two or more non consecutive tasks may be linked using the Linking function,
- Select non adjacent tasks to be linked by Ctl clicking on the Gantt Chart bar or **Line Number**, not the **Task Name**, or
- Click and drag on tasks that are next to each other,
- Click on the **Link** tasks toolbar button and the tasks will be linked with a Finish to Start link,
- **Note:** This function ignores the order that the tasks are selected in and only links from top to bottom for the selected tasks. P6 and Microsoft Project that link in the order they were selected.

130

Link Task Mode

- This function is enabled by clicking on the **Link Task Mode** icon or **Ctl+F3**, which is probably simpler,

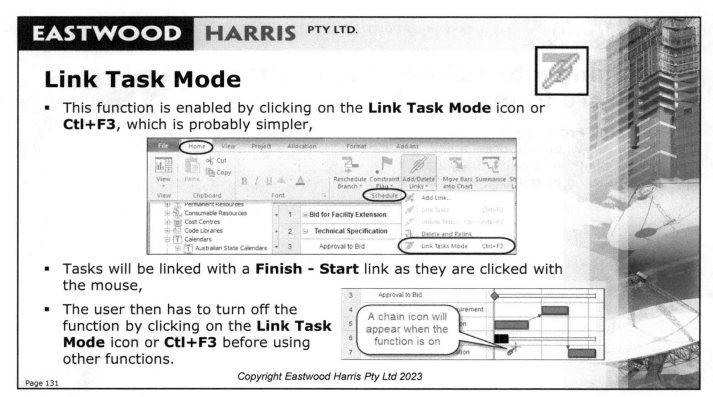

- Tasks will be linked with a **Finish - Start** link as they are clicked with the mouse,

- The user then has to turn off the function by clicking on the **Link Task Mode** icon or **Ctl+F3** before using other functions.

A chain icon will appear when the function is on

Page 131

131

Editing and Deleting Links

- A selected link is green and may be deleted by pressing the **Delete** key or using the **Unlink Task** button,

- Links may be edited in the **Link Properties** form which may be opened by:

  - Selecting the link and then right clicking and selecting Properties,

  - Opening the **Bar and Task Properties** form or view,

  - Clicking in a **Predecessor** or **Successor** column cell,

  - Successor Links may be reassigned to another task by dragging, see next slide,

- To deselect a link, click elsewhere in the Bar Chart.

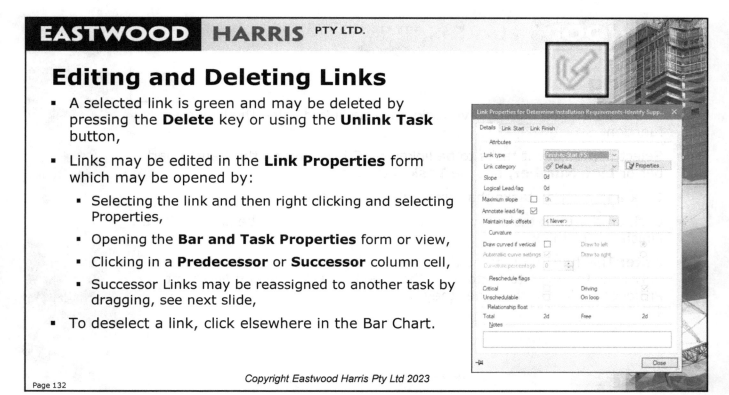

Page 132

132

Moving Successor Links

- When a link has the incorrect successor it may be 'dragged' with the mouse to the correct task and does not need to be deleted and redrawn, as with P6 and Microsoft project,

  - Click on the link to select it and it will go green,

  - Hover the cursor over the end of the link you wish the move until a 'cross' cursor becomes visible,

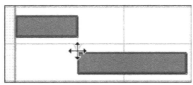

  - The link successor may be dragged to the correct successor.

133

Reviewing Logic using Tables

- Logic may be reviewed in Tables with predecessor and/or successor columns,

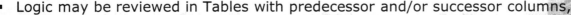

- Powerproject has many more option in the **Table Definition** form than other products for reviewing link information in columns,

- This includes the task **Name** or **ID** or **Line Number** and **Lead** and **Lag** details by selecting **All Details** or **Link Notes** or **Link Category**.

134

EASTWOOD HARRIS PTY LTD.

Percent Lead and Lag

- Double clicking on a Link will open the **Link Properties** form where Links may be edited,

- One interesting function of Powerproject is the ability to enter a **Percent lag**, which is available in Microsoft Project but not P6,

- Thus the Lead or Lag duration changes in proportion to the Task Duration,

- **Note:** If all leads and lags are entered as a Percentage this may allow a **Monte Carlo** evaluation to be performed on a schedule.

Page 135   *Copyright Eastwood Harris Pty Ltd 2023*

135

EASTWOOD HARRIS PTY LTD.

Navigate the Logic and Editing Links

- You may use the **Bar and Task Properties**, **Links** tab of the dialog box to navigate through the logic of your project,

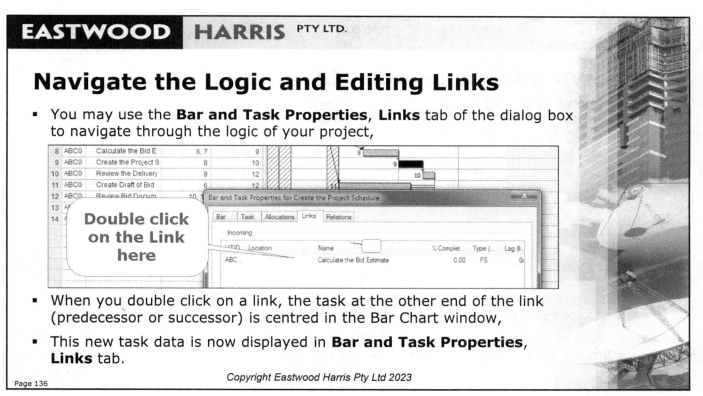

Double click on the Link here

- When you double click on a link, the task at the other end of the link (predecessor or successor) is centred in the Bar Chart window,

- This new task data is now displayed in **Bar and Task Properties**, **Links** tab.

Page 136   *Copyright Eastwood Harris Pty Ltd 2023*

136

EASTWOOD HARRIS PTY LTD.

Split Windows and Linking

Links may be created between tasks when two windows are created and tiled one above the other, to do this:

- Create a second tab using the **View**, **Tab**, **New Tab** command,

- Tile the tabs horizontally using the **View**, **Tab**, **Tile Horizontally** command,

- Drag the links from one task to another in the other window,

- This is a neat method of linking tasks that are in different parts of the schedule.

This Link is being dragged from one window to another

Page 137

137

EASTWOOD HARRIS PTY LTD.

Reviewing Logic using the Network Viewer

- The **Network Viewer** is used to review the logic and other project data,

- This is often referred to as a **Network Diagram** or a **PERT** diagram,

- The button to view the **Network** is found on the **Ribbon** toolbar under **Project**, **Data**.

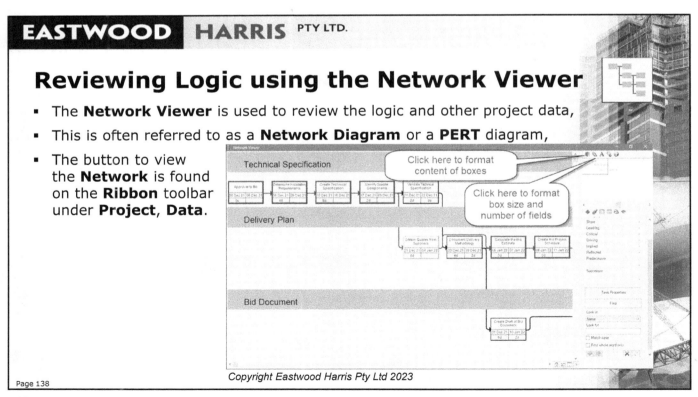

Page 138

138

EASTWOOD HARRIS PTY LTD.

Reschedule

- When you have linked your tasks you may **Reschedule** the project,

- If you have **Reschedule** set to **Automatic** under the **Reschedule Options** then you will not need to reschedule,

- The **Reschedule** option performs a series of **Critical Path** calculations:

  - Calculates the **Early Dates**,

  - Calculates the **Late Dates**,

  - Calculates **Total Float**,

  - Calculates **Free Float**,

  - Calculates the earliest project end date.

Reschedule Progress Period Warning ✕

Straighten progress period

The reschedule will straighten the progress line to this period: [Progress entry period ⌄]

Progress entry period

Progress is being recorded against this progress period: [Project Report Date (6/12/2021 00:0(⌄]

☐ Do not warn again

[OK] [Cancel]

Copyright Eastwood Harris Pty Ltd 2023

EASTWOOD HARRIS PTY LTD.

To Reschedule the Whole Project:

- If you do not have **Automatic schedule** set and after making changes one would normally **Reschedule** the whole project,

- To **Reschedule** the whole project:

  - Click the **Reschedule All** tool bar button, or

  - Press the **F9** button,

- Accept the defaults, and press **OK**,

- The project critical path is shown outlined in red.

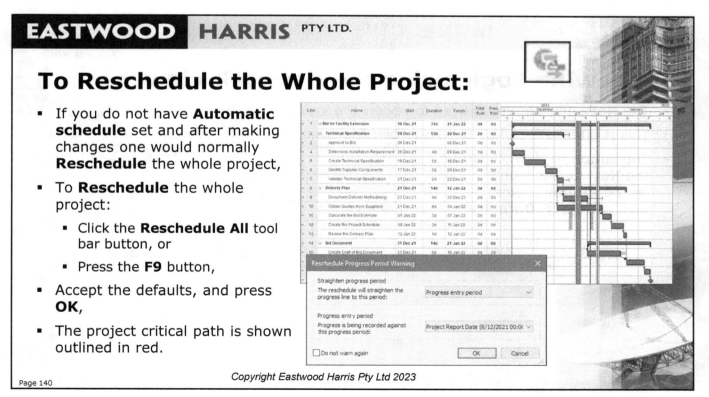

Copyright Eastwood Harris Pty Ltd 2023

© *Eastwood Harris Pty Ltd 2024*

This publication is only sold as a bound book and no parts may be reproduced by any means, electronic or print.

EASTWOOD HARRIS PTY LTD.

Reschedule Options

There are several options for rescheduling:

- **Reschedule Branch** reschedules tasks in the current view and any out of view subordinate tasks,

- **Reschedule View** reschedules tasks in the applied view but does not schedule tasks in **Expanded** or **Summary** tasks that are closed,

- **Reschedule All** reschedules all tasks,

- **Reschedule Selection** reschedules the selected task or tasks.

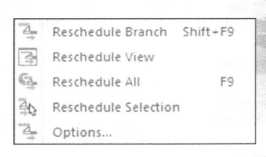

	Reschedule Branch	Shift+F9
	Reschedule View	
	Reschedule All	F9
	Reschedule Selection	
	Options...	

Page 141

141

EASTWOOD HARRIS PTY LTD.

Understanding the File, Options, Reschedule form

- The **File**, **Options**, **Reschedule** form has some features not seen in other software, which we will not cover in this course,

- The **Auto reschedule** section allows manual or automatic scheduling,

- **Straighten progress line to period** will be covered in the Updating modules,

- Help files explains how these function operate:

  - **Tasks with no links**

  - **Tasks with only outgoing links**

  - **Compatibility**

  - **Options**

  - **Compute**

- The options set in the picture will result in the schedule calculating in a similar way to P6 and Microsoft Project.

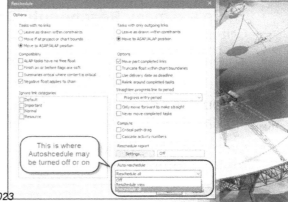

This is where Autoshcedule may be turned off or on

Page 142

142

Reschedule Report

- The **Reschedule Report** is useful to review when you have a large schedule,

- You may select to run the **Reschedule Report** from the **File**, **Options**, **Reschedule** form, **Settings** button,

- The **Reschedule Report Settings** form will open and is used to tailor the report content,

- The **Reschedule Report** may be displayed in a browser or saved as a report,

- The **Reschedule Report Warning** form will appear when you reschedule confirming you would like to view the **Reschedule Report**.

Page 143

Copyright Eastwood Harris Pty Ltd 2023

143

6 - LINKING TASKS TO CREATE A CRITICAL PATH SCHEDULE - SUMMARY

- This module covered how to link tasks to create a critical path program, and

- Rescheduling a project,

- There are many **Reschedule Options** and some will not produce a Critical Path program,

- This course will not cover these options in detail but feel free to explore then in your own time,

- If you use the setting I recommend then the schedule will calculate in a similar way to other products and will create a Critical Path schedule,

- Once we have covered adding constraints we will have covered all the topics required to create a schedule in Powerproject.

Page 144

Copyright Eastwood Harris Pty Ltd 2023

144

EASTWOOD HARRIS PTY LTD.

Workshop 6 – Adding the Links and Reschedule

- You have determined the logical sequence of tasks, so you may now enter the links,

- After you have entered the links you should reschedule the program by pressing F9 if you do not have **Auto reschedule** switched on and this will calculate the Start and Finish dates and Total and Free floats.

Page 145

145

EASTWOOD HARRIS PTY LTD.

7 – CONSTRAINTS

In this module we look at :

- How to add and remove constraints,
- Snapping
- Start on a New Day
- Partial Critical Path
- Float display and
- Negative float applies to chain.

Page 146

146

EASTWOOD HARRIS PTY LTD.

Understanding Constraints

- To correctly model the impact of events outside the logical sequence, you should use constraints,

- A constraint would be imposed to specific dates such as:

    - The availability of a facility to allow work to commence, or

    - The predetermined time a project must be complete by,

- Constraints in a schedule should be cross-referenced to Milestone Dates found in supporting documentation such as contract documentation or scope documents using **Task Notes** Function.

Copyright Eastwood Harris Pty Ltd 2023

Page 147

147

EASTWOOD HARRIS PTY LTD.

Setting and Removing Constraints

- Constraints may be set on either the Start or Finish of tasks,

- To set a constraint when **Auto rescheduling** is not set:

    - Move the task to the required date position,

    - Right click on the task and select **Constraint Flag**,

    - Select the type of constraint from the list,

- A flag will appear on the task,

- To remove an existing constraint,

    - Select the constraint,

    - Right click and select **Remove**.

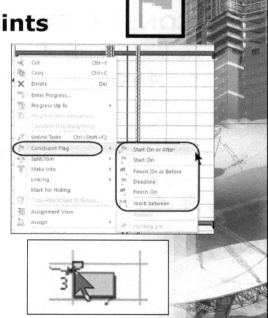

Copyright Eastwood Harris Pty Ltd 2023

Page 148

148

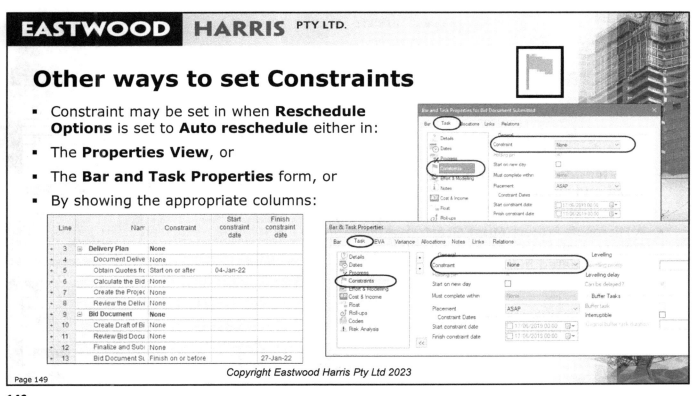

Other ways to set Constraints

- Constraint may be set in when **Reschedule Options** is set to **Auto reschedule** either in:
- The **Properties View**, or
- The **Bar and Task Properties** form, or
- By showing the appropriate columns:

Line		Name	Constraint	Start constraint date	Finish constraint date
3	☐	Delivery Plan	None		
4		Document Delive	None		
5		Obtain Quotes fro	Start on or after	04-Jan-22	
6		Calculate the Bid	None		
7		Create the Projec	None		
8		Review the Delive	None		
9	☐	Bid Document	None		
10		Create Draft of Bi	None		
11		Review Bid Docu	None		
12		Finalize and Subr	None		
13		Bid Document Su	Finish on or before		27-Jan-22

Copyright Eastwood Harris Pty Ltd 2023

Page 149

149

Types of Constraint

- A **Holding Pin** calculates like like an **Early Start** constraint:
  - It moves forward with the task but not backwards, when it is scheduled, or
  - Moves with the task when manually moved by dragging,
- A **Hard Constraint** means that the task is scheduled on that date and **Negative Float** is created on the predecessor when the predecessor finishes later than the **Hard Constraint** date,
- See picture on the next slide:

Picture	Link Name	Link Type
🚩	Start on or after	Soft
🚩	Start on	Hard
🏴	Finish on or before	Soft
🏴	Deadline	Soft
🏴	Finish on	Hard
🚩	Work (schedule) between	Soft
📌	Holding pin	Moves with the task when manually moved

Copyright Eastwood Harris Pty Ltd 2023

Page 150

150

Constraint Calculation

All products calculate differently,

- Powerproject **Start On** is a **Hard Constraint**,

- A P6 **Mandatory Start** is also **Hard** and calculates like a Powerproject **Start On**,

- A Microsoft Project **Must Start On** constraint is **Soft**, negative float is created but the tasks acknowledges the predecessor.

Start	Finish	Constraint	Start constraint date	Total float	
10 Jul 23	14 Jul 23	None		-2d	
13 Jul 23	17 Jul 23	Start on	13-Jul-23	0d	

Start	Finish	Primary Constraint Date	Primary Constraint	Total Float	
10-Jul-23 08	14-Jul-23 16			-2d	
13-Jul-23 08*	17-Jul-23 16	13-Jul-23 08	Mandatory Start	0d	

Start	Finish	Constraint Date	Constraint Type	Total Slack	
10 Jul '23	14 Jul '23	NA	As Soon As Possible	-2d	
17 Jul '23	19 Jul '23	13 Jul '23	Must Start On	-2d	

Page 151

Copyright Eastwood Harris Pty Ltd 2023

151

As Late As Possible – Placement...

- In Oracle Primavera P6 and Microsoft Project, to make a task **As Late As Possible** (ALAP) then the task is assigned as a Constraint,

    - P6 is not a true ALAP calculation as it consumes **Free Float** and will not delay successor activities and would normally be called a **Zero Free Float** constraint,

    - Powerproject **ALAP Placement** calculates in the same way as P6 and consumes **Free Float** only and does not delay successor tasks,

    - Microsoft Project is a true **ALAP** constraint and will delay all successors with **Total Float** consume successor **Total Float**,

- Powerproject allows a **Placement** option in the **Properties**, **Task**, **Constraints** tab:

    - **ASAP** – As Soon As Possible

    - **ALAP** – Zero Free Float

    - **ASAP Force Critical** – This sets the Early dates to equal the late dates and makes the task Critical.

Page 152

Copyright Eastwood Harris Pty Ltd 2023

152

As Late As Possible - Placement

In the picture below:

- Task 1 creates Total Float and Free Float for Task 5,
- Task 5 has a Start No Earlier Than Constraint,
- Task 2 is **ASAP** and has both Total Float and Free Float
- Task 3 is **ALAP** does not delay Task 5 which still has Total Float,
- Task 4 **ASAP Force Critical** and has no Total Float or Free Float:

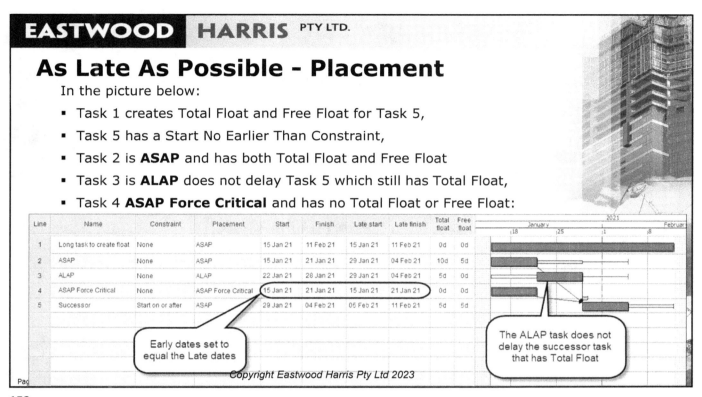

Copyright Eastwood Harris Pty Ltd 2023

153

Start on a New Day and Snapping

- **Start on new day**, forces a task to start on a new day,
  - This is very useful for tasks like Concrete Pours which should not be commenced towards the end of a day:

- **Snapping**, make all task durations round to a unit,
  - This is very useful to prevent tasks durations in fractions of a day when updating tasks with a percent complete,
  - Select **View**, **Show** to set the snapping unit,
  - The author normally uses Days on construction projects.

Copyright Eastwood Harris Pty Ltd 2023

Page 154

154

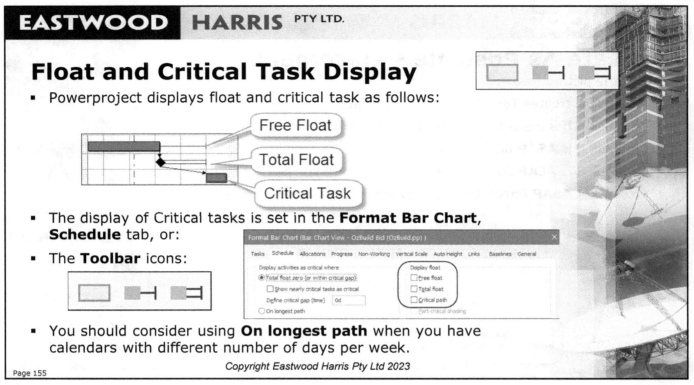

Float and Critical Task Display

- Powerproject displays float and critical task as follows:

  - Free Float
  - Total Float
  - Critical Task

- The display of Critical tasks is set in the **Format Bar Chart**, **Schedule** tab, or:

- The **Toolbar** icons:

- You should consider using **On longest path** when you have calendars with different number of days per week.

Page 155

155

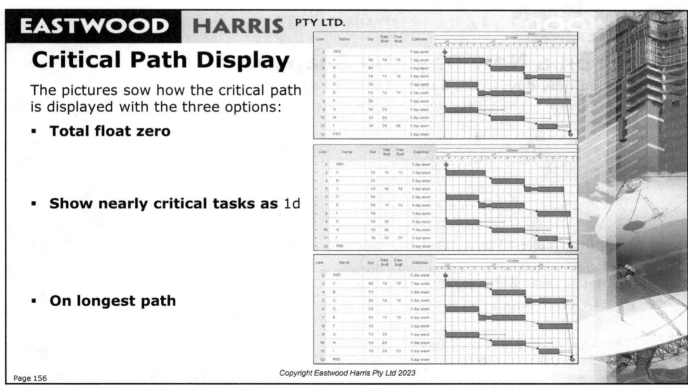

Critical Path Display

The pictures sow how the critical path is displayed with the three options:

- **Total float zero**

- **Show nearly critical tasks as** 1d

- **On longest path**

Page 156

156

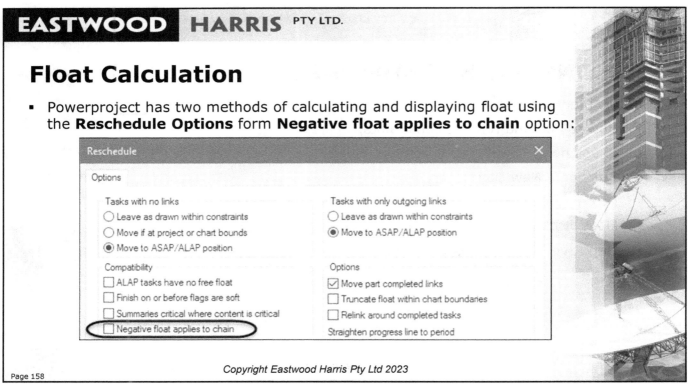

Partial Critical Path

- A **Partial Critical Path** identifies critical and non-critical portions of a task,

- A **Partial Critical Path** may be displayed when **Mid Links** are used,

- To display a **Partial Critical Path** two conditions must be met in the **Format Bar Chart** form:

    - The **Non-Work**ing tab, **On tasks** unchecked, and

    - The **Schedule** tab, **Partial critical shading checked**.

Float Calculation

- Powerproject has two methods of calculating and displaying float using the **Reschedule Options** form **Negative float applies to chain** option:

EASTWOOD HARRIS PTY LTD.

Float Calculation

- **Negative float applies to chain option** unchecked:
  - Only the first task in a chain causing negative float is displayed with Negative Float and it also displays a Negative Float bar:

Line	Name	Start	Duration	Finish	Total float	Free float
1	Obtain Quotes from Suppliers	30-Dec-21	8d	11-Jan-22	-2d	0d

- **Negative float applies to chain option** checked:
  - All tasks in the chain calculate Negative Float but **NO** Negative Float bar is displayed against any task,
  - This is how P6 and Microsoft Project calculate, but they will both display a Negative Float bar,
  - Powerproject does NOT display a **Negative Float** bar with this option.

Line	Name	Start	Duration	Finish	Total float	Free float
1	Delivery Plan	23-Dec-21	19d	21-Jan-22	-2d	0d
2	Obtain Quotes from Suppliers	04-Jan-22	8d	13-Jan-22	-2d	0d
3	Calculate the Bid Estimate	14-Jan-22	3d	17-Jan-22	-2d	0d
4	Create the Project Schedule	18-Jan-22	3d	20-Jan-22	-2d	0d
5	Review the Delivery Plan	21-Jan-22	1d	21-Jan-22	-2d	0d
6	Review Bid Document	24-Jan-22	4d	27-Jan-22	-2d	0d
7	Finalize and Submit Bid Document	28-Jan-22	2d	31-Jan-22	-2d	0d
8	Bid Document Submitted	31-Jan-22		31-Jan-22	-2d	0d

EASTWOOD HARRIS PTY LTD.

7 – CONSTRAINTS SUMMARY

In this module we looked at

- How to add and remove constraints,
- Snapping
- Start on a New Day
- Partial Critical Path
- Float display and
- Negative float applies to chain.

EASTWOOD HARRIS PTY LTD.

Workshop 7 - Constraints

- Management has provided further input to your schedule,
- You will need to set some constraints and eliminate Negative Float.

Page 161

161

EASTWOOD HARRIS PTY LTD.

8 - OTHER TASK TYPES

This module will cover the following topics:

- Task-per-line mode
- Expanded Tasks
- Hammock Tasks
- Subheadings and
- Buffer Tasks.

Page 162

162

EASTWOOD HARRIS PTY LTD.

Task-per-line mode

- Powerproject may display multiple tasks on line in the Gantt Chart,

- Powerproject terms this **Multiple Tasks on a Bar**,

- This is useful when it is desirable to reduce the number of lines in a program and when it would be logical to display them all on the same line,

- Powerproject may also display these tasks on separate lines if required,

- The picture below is an example of a housing project with each line representing a house with each trade represented by the tasks:

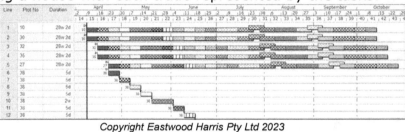

Copyright Eastwood Harris Pty Ltd 2023

Page 163

163

EASTWOOD HARRIS PTY LTD.

Understanding Bars and Tasks

- When you create multiple tasks on one line the two terms you need to understand are **Bar** and **Task**,

- A **Bar** contains one or more **Tasks**:

  - **The Bar Name** is displayed in the **Name** column when the Tasks are rolled up,

Line	Name	Bar name	Task name	Dur
1	Concrete Pour	Concrete Pour	Form,Pour,Reo,Strip	12d

- **Tasks** may be drawn on the Gantt Chart:

  - There may be multiple **Tasks** to a **Bar**,

  - The **Task Name** is displayed in the **Name** column a multiple Task is expanded.

Line	Name	Bar name	Task name	Dur
1	Form	Concrete Pour	Form	5d
2	Pour	Concrete Pour	Pour	1d
3	Reo	Concrete Pour	Reo	5d
4	Strip	Concrete Pour	Strip	1d

Copyright Eastwood Harris Pty Ltd 2023

Page 164

164

EASTWOOD HARRIS PTY LTD.

Adding Task-per-line

- You may create multiple tasks on one line by dragging in the Gantt Chart and then enter the **Bar** name in the **Name** column:

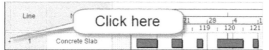

- Click the "+" button to the left of the line number within the table and enter each **Task** name in the **Name** column,

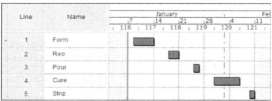

- Click the "-" button to return the tasks to one line mode.

Page 165

165

EASTWOOD HARRIS PTY LTD.

Understand the Difference Between Bars and Task

- When there are multiple Tasks-per-line:

  - The **Bar** description is seen in the **Name** column when the tasks **ARE** on one line,

  - The **Task** description is seen in the **Name** column when the tasks **ARE** NOT on one line,

  - The **Bar** description is Concrete Slab,

  - The **Tasks** are Form, Reo, Pour etc.:

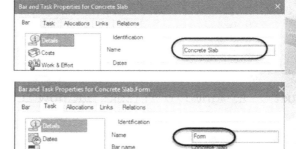

Page 166

166

EASTWOOD HARRIS PTY LTD.

Task-per-line "Inherited Links"

- By default Tasks on one line have an inherited Finish-to-Start link between tasks and no link is required, and the tasks will run consecutively,

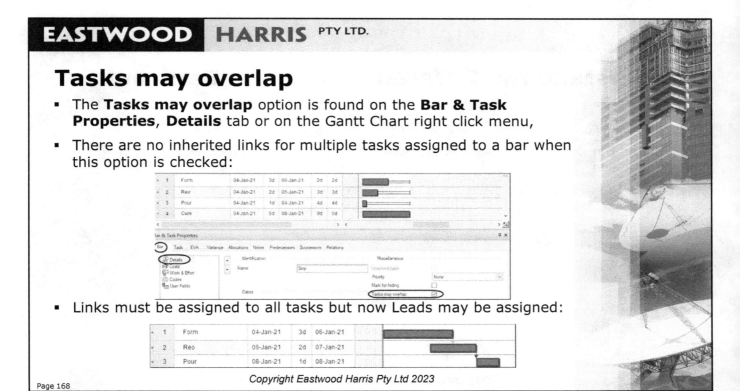

- **Note:** This mode may not be considered a **Critical Path** schedule as tasks are not linked,

- It is possible to draw links between tasks on the same bar but this will ensure a delay or interval between them,

- **Note**: **Negative Lags** will not calculate unless the **Bar** option **Tasks may Overlap** is checked, see next slide.

Page 167

167

EASTWOOD HARRIS PTY LTD.

Tasks may overlap

- The **Tasks may overlap** option is found on the **Bar & Task Properties**, **Details** tab or on the Gantt Chart right click menu,

- There are no inherited links for multiple tasks assigned to a bar when this option is checked:

- Links must be assigned to all tasks but now Leads may be assigned:

Page 168

168

EASTWOOD HARRIS PTY LTD.

Tasks May Overlap examples...

- Therefore if you wish multiple tasks on one line to overlap then select the Bar and right click in the Gantt Chart area and select **Tasks may Overlap**,

- Multiple task on one line **NOT** summarised:

- Multiple task on one line summarised:

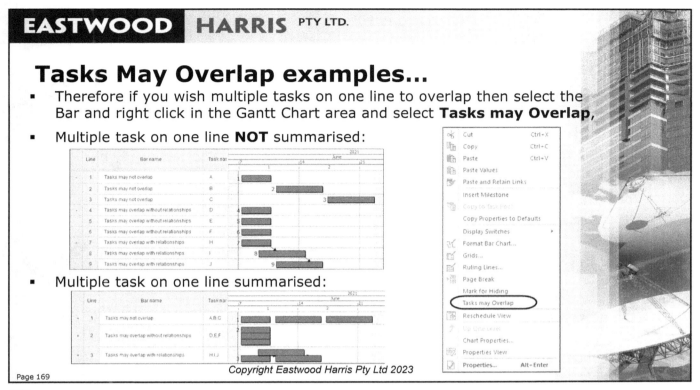

Copyright Eastwood Harris Pty Ltd 2023

Page 169

169

EASTWOOD HARRIS PTY LTD.

Tasks May Overlap examples

- Tasks may be added to a Bar using the **Roll tasks up** function,

- In the example the Bar Name was changes to "Concrete Pour",

- These Tasks are added as Tasks may overlap,

- The **Unroll tasks** may be used to remove Tasks from Bars.

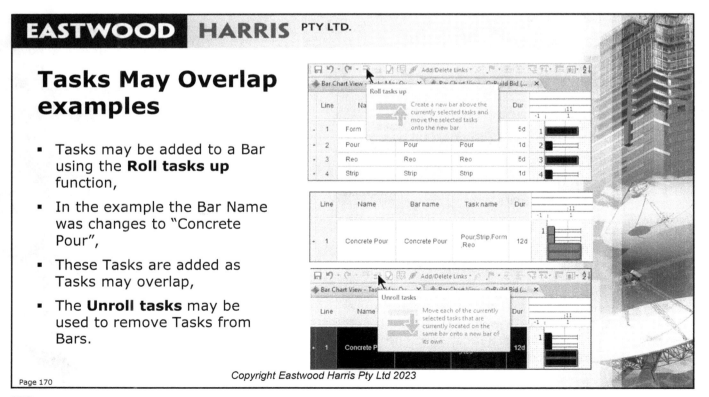

Copyright Eastwood Harris Pty Ltd 2023

Page 170

170

EASTWOOD HARRIS PTY LTD.

Expanded Tasks

- **Expanded** tasks allow detailed planning to be hidden in turn allowing the uncluttering of a view with the detail readily available,

- They **DO NOT** operate like Microsoft Project Summary Tasks or P6 Hammocks,

- Expanded tasks are displayed as a normal task but the detailed tasks may be hidden and are held in a **Sub Chart**,

- The **Project View** displays **Expanded Tasks** nodes:

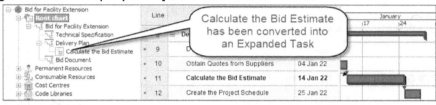

- Existing tasks may be converted into **Expanded** tasks and detail added below them or on new ones created,

- Tasks under an **Expanded Task** are called **Subtasks**.

171

EASTWOOD HARRIS PTY LTD.

Creating Expanded Tasks...

- To create an **Expanded** task either:

  - Create a new task in the normal way, or

  - Select an existing task,

- Place the mouse over the task in the Gantt Chart and right click,

- Select **Make into**, **Expanded**,

- At this point in time you may create detailed tasks under the **Expanded Task** and

- These new tasks are called **Sub tasks** that are held in a **Sub Chart**, which may be linked and resources allocated in the normal way.

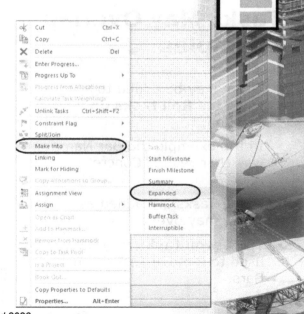

172

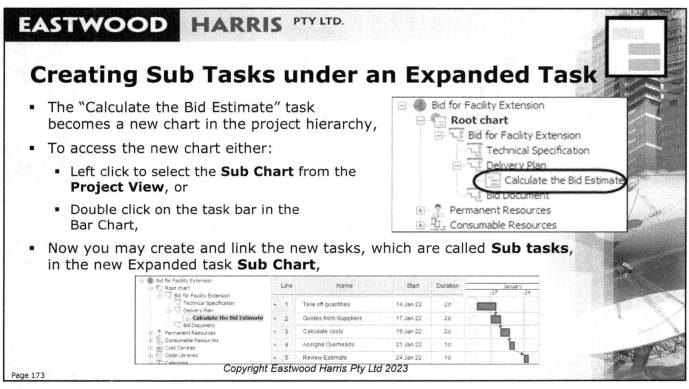

Page 173

173

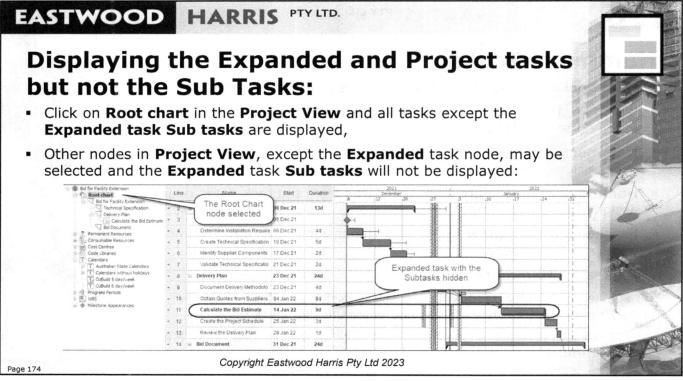

Page 174

174

EASTWOOD HARRIS PTY LTD.

Displaying Expanded tasks Sub tasks and Project tasks together:

- Select the required nodes in the **Project View** in order to display the **Expanded** tasks **Sub tasks** with other project tasks on one screen,

- Now all tasks associated with the selected nodes are displayed and links may be made between any tasks:

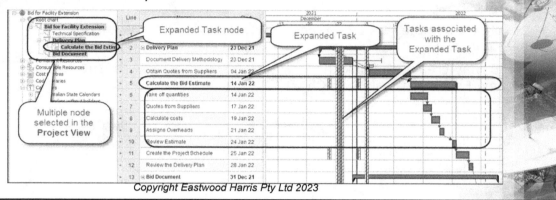

Page 175   *Copyright Eastwood Harris Pty Ltd 2023*

175

EASTWOOD HARRIS PTY LTD.

Hammock

Hammock Tasks

- **Hammocks** are used to summarise tasks that are not adjacent to each other,

- Unlike P6, Powerproject **Hammock** tasks do not have **Links** to the tasks assigned to the **Hammock**,

- **Hammock** start and finish dates are taken from the earliest and latest dates of their assigned tasks,

- **Hammock** durations are back calculated from the task dates over the calendar assigned to the Hammock,

- Expanding a **Hammock** will display the assigned tasks twice, in the chart and under the hammock,

- To create a **Hammock**, either:

  - Select an empty bar of your project by clicking on the line number, then select **Home, Insert – Hammock**, and enter the Hammock name, or

  - Draw a task, name it and then Right Click on the bar and select **Make into, Hammock**.

Page 176   *Copyright Eastwood Harris Pty Ltd 2023*

176

EASTWOOD HARRIS PTY LTD.

Assigning tasks to a Hammock:

To assign Tasks to a Hammock

- Select the tasks to be added to a **Hammock**,

- Right click and select **Add to Hammock...**,

- Select the required **Hammock** and click **OK**,

- Tasks may be assigned to multiple **Hammocks**,

- **Hammock** tasks are displayed in two places:

  - In its original position, and

  - A copy of the task is displayed under the hammock when it is expanded by clicking on the + by the Name:

- To remove tasks from a **Hammock**,

  - Right click on the task and

  - Select **Remove from Hammock**.

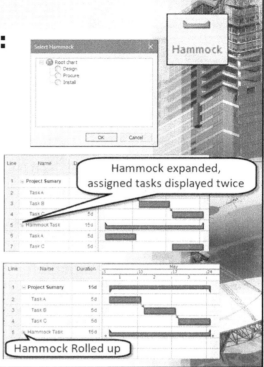

Copyright Eastwood Harris Pty Ltd 2023

Page 177

177

EASTWOOD HARRIS PTY LTD.

Subheadings

- A **Subheading** is a **Bar Name** without tasks,

- A task name may be entered and no task bar drawn on the Gantt Chart or duration entered,

Line	Name	Start	Duration	Finish	May	June
1	First Task Name	20/05/19	3d	22/05/19	1	
2	Second Task	24/05/19	1w 2d	03/06/19	2	
	SUB HEADING					
3	Third Task	03/06/19	1w 3d	12/06/19	3	
4	Fourth Task	14/06/19	3d	18/06/19		4

- This text then becomes a **Subheading**,

- This is useful if you have a long list of tasks under a Summary task and you do not want to add any more lower level Summary tasks, but you want to group them under headings,

- **Note**: A **Subheading** may also be created by a band heading create by grouping tasks by a code.

Copyright Eastwood Harris Pty Ltd 2023

Page 178

178

EASTWOOD HARRIS PTY LTD.

Buffer Tasks

- **Buffer tasks** are used to show and manage the contingent time,
- Their duration is self adjusting,
- There are two types of buffer tasks:
  - **Feeder buffers** – which sit within the project protecting key dates, and
  - **Project buffers** – which are usually the last task in a project protecting the project end date,
- A buffer contributes to the Critical Path calculation, but when its start date is affected and it will shrink (or expand) and protect the Critical Path,
- This technique is often referred to as **Critical Chain Scheduling**, see **Eli Goldratt's** book titled **Theory of Constraints**,
- **Note:** This method of planning is supported by the Society of Construction Laws' – Delay and Disruption Protocol – October 2002 (see www.scl.org.uk).

Page 179   *Copyright Eastwood Harris Pty Ltd 2023*

179

EASTWOOD HARRIS PTY LTD.

How to create a Buffer Task

- To create a **Buffer task**,
  - Create a task in the normal way,
  - Link the task into the project and reschedule the project so the tasks have the correct dates,
  - Right Click on the task and select to **Make into, Buffer Task**.

Page 180   *Copyright Eastwood Harris Pty Ltd 2023*

180

EASTWOOD HARRIS PTY LTD.

8 - OTHER TASK TYPES SUMMARY

In this module we covered the following topics:

- Task-per-line mode
- Expanded Tasks
- Hammock Tasks
- Subheadings and
- Buffer Tasks.

EASTWOOD HARRIS PTY LTD.

Workshop 8 – Other Task Types

- This workshop will take you through the process of creating the following in your schedule:
    - Task-per-line mode
    - Expanded Tasks
    - Hammock Tasks
    - Subheadings where Bar Names are used as Headers Only
- Before you move on to the next workshop delete all of the tasks you create in this workshop.

EASTWOOD HARRIS PTY LTD.

9 - FORMATTING THE DISPLAY

We will cover in this module formatting:

- The Date Zone, Gridlines, Vertical Shading and Multiple Date Zones,
- Hiding non-working time,
- Formatting bars and Links,
- Adding Notes,
- Link Categories,
- Columns, Date and Durations,
- Tables and Views,
- Adding Annotations,
- Task Numbering and
- Timeline View.

EASTWOOD HARRIS PTY LTD.

Introduction to Views

- Project data is displayed using a **View** and any formatting changes are editing a **View**, or an attribute associated to **View**, such as a **Table**, **Filter** or **Sort/Group**,

- A **View** holds the following formatting:
    - **Date Zone**
    - **Gantt Chart**

- Other attributes associated with a **View**, such as **Tables**, **Filters** or **Sort/Groups** may be assigned to multiple views, and edited without the associated view being displayed,

- **Note:** The **Undo** button does not undo formatting changes, only calculations and data changes.

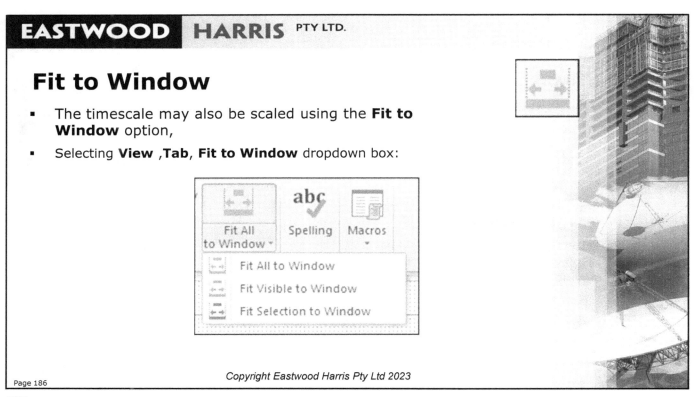

EASTWOOD HARRIS PTY LTD.

Editing Date Zone Rulers

- Up to 10 **Date Zone Rulers** may be displayed,

- The picture is displaying 6,

- To format the **Date Zone** Rulers:

    - Open the **Date Zone Propertie**s form, **General** tab,

    - Add or remove **Rulers** from the right hand side of the by selecting the desired scale under **Type**,

    - Then select **Time Unit** and **Quantity**, and

    - Reformat the display using **Background**, **Tick Marks**, **Text** and **Font** from the form.

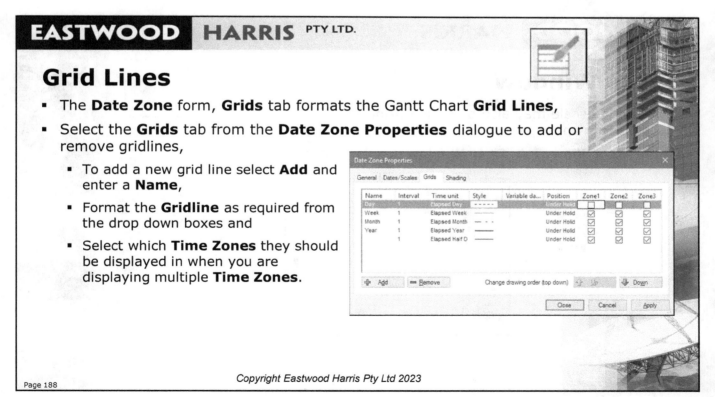

Page 187

187

EASTWOOD HARRIS PTY LTD.

Grid Lines

- The **Date Zone** form, **Grids** tab formats the Gantt Chart **Grid Lines**,

- Select the **Grids** tab from the **Date Zone Properties** dialogue to add or remove gridlines,

    - To add a new grid line select **Add** and enter a **Name**,

    - Format the **Gridline** as required from the drop down boxes and

    - Select which **Time Zones** they should be displayed in when you are displaying multiple **Time Zones**.

Page 188

188

EASTWOOD HARRIS PTY LTD.

Day, Week and Month Numbering

- Powerproject allows **Day**, **Week** or **Month** numbering using the **Elapsed units** option in the **Date Zone Properties** form, **General** tab:

- The **Date Zero** is where numbering is commenced and will default to the **Project start date** when the project is created,

- To align **Date Zero** to another date:
    - Open the **Date Zone Properties** form,
    - Select the **Dates/Scales** tab,
    - Select the **Date Zero** from the drop box,
    - Select **Close**.

Page 189

Copyright Eastwood Harris Pty Ltd 2023

189

EASTWOOD HARRIS PTY LTD.

Vertical Shading

- The **Date Zone** form, **Shading** tab formats the Gantt Chart,

- Like P6, vertical shading may be placed behind the tasks to represent Shut Down time etc., to add shading:
    - Select the **Date Zone Properties** form **Shading** tab,
    - Select **Add** to add a Shading,
    - Enter the **Shading Start** and **Finish** dates or a **Variable Date** from the list and format the colour:

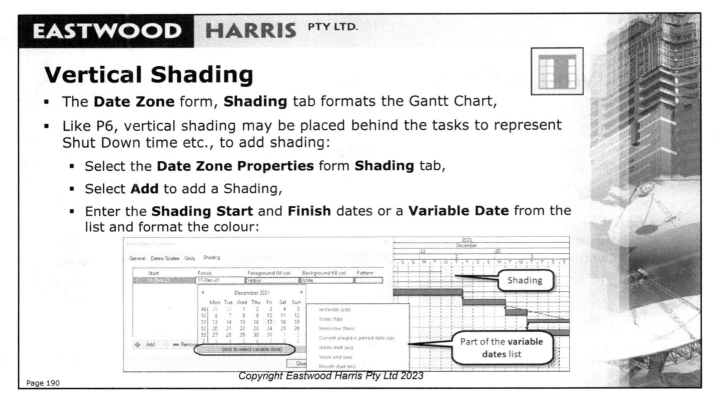

Page 190

Copyright Eastwood Harris Pty Ltd 2023

190

EASTWOOD HARRIS PTY LTD.

Multiple Date Zones

- The **Date Zone** may be divided into two or three different zones each with a different scales,

						2004	
	January					February	
5	12	19	26	2	9	16	23
1	1	2	3	4	5	6	7

- This is similar to the **SureTrak Zoomed Timescale** function,
  - Place the mouse in the **Date Zone** where you want the second or third new **Date Zone** to start,
  - Right click and select **Start New Scale Zone**,
- A grey line will indicate the start of the new **Date Zone**,
- Now each time scale may be formatted individually,
- To remove **Zone 2** or **Zone 3**, right click in the **Date Zone** and select to **Remove This Scale Zone**.

Page 191

191

EASTWOOD HARRIS PTY LTD.

Displaying and Hiding non-working time

- Powerproject allows non working time to be hidden and this is termed by Powerproject as **Folded Out of View**,
- It is often best to ensure that **Non Working** time is not displayed but you need to ensure your **Folding Calendar** does not fold work time out of view,
- Thus if you have 5d/w and a 6d/w calendars, then make the **Folding Calendar** the 6d/w calendar,
- Examples on the next slide.

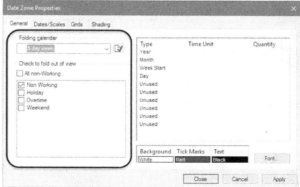

Page 192

192

EASTWOOD HARRIS PTY LTD.

Hiding non-working time examples

- No working time hidden and timescale shows full 24 hours: **Note: Driving Links** are not vertical,

- **Non-Working** time hidden, so only 08:00 to 16:00 is displayed and **Driving Links** become vertical:

- Weekends hidden on a 5 day/week **Folding calendar**:

- Holidays hidden:

Page 193

193

EASTWOOD HARRIS PTY LTD.

Formatting the Bar Chart

- Powerproject formatting is in most areas more functional than P6 and Microsoft Project and in a few areas less,

- For example Powerproject links may be coloured and non work time displayed according to each tasks' calendar, but Float bars and the Critical Path may not be formatted, just displayed or hidden,

- Most formatting options are on the **Format** tab,

- When the icon has a highlighted background the attribute is being displayed:

Page 194

194

Format Bar Chart form, Tasks tab

- Most bar formatting options are found in the **Format Bar Chart** form,
- This form is opened by right clicking in the Gant Chart and selecting the **Format Bar Chart** command,
- The **Tasks** tab is used to format the Gantt Chart task bars.

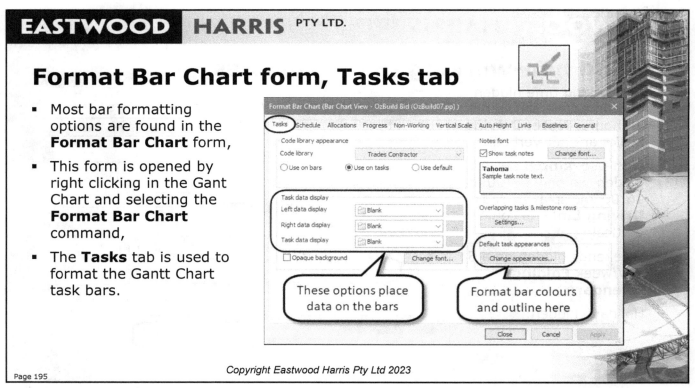

195

Adding Task Notes and Dated Task Notes

- **Task Notes** may be recorded in either:
  - The **Bar and Task Properties** form, **Task** tab, **Notes** section, or
  - The **Bar and Task Properties View**, **Notes** tab,
- **Notes** are typed in the **Notes** heading, or
- **Dated notes** are created by right clicking to open a menu and may be either:
  - A **Text Note** with a **Title** and **Details**, or
  - A **File Note** with a link to a file, or
  - A **URL Note** with a link to a URL,
- A **Dated Notes** may also be created by the **Site Progress** tool, and
- Deleted by **Right clicking**.

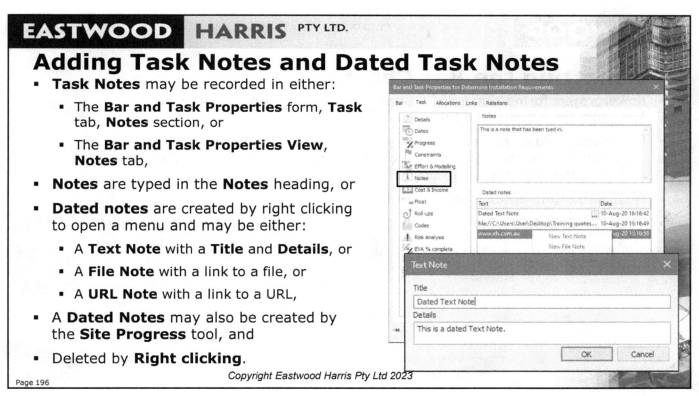

196

Displaying Task Notes

- When the **Format Bar Chart** form, **Task** tab, **Show task notes** check box is checked then a yellow indicator is displayed in the top right corner of a task bar indicating a task has been assigned either a **Note** or a **Dated Text Note** and

- When there are multiple **Task Notes** then only the first **Task Note** is displayed in a pop up window when the cursor is placed on the task,

- **URL Notes** and **File Notes** do not display a yellow indicator.

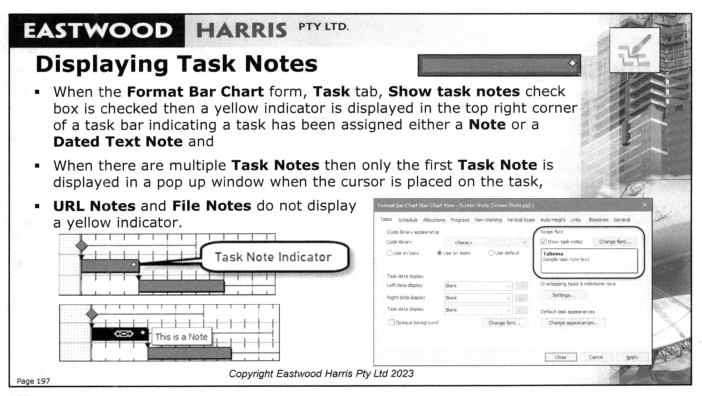

197

Format Bar Chart, Schedule tab

- **Free float**, **Total float** and **Critical path check** boxes hide or display these bars:

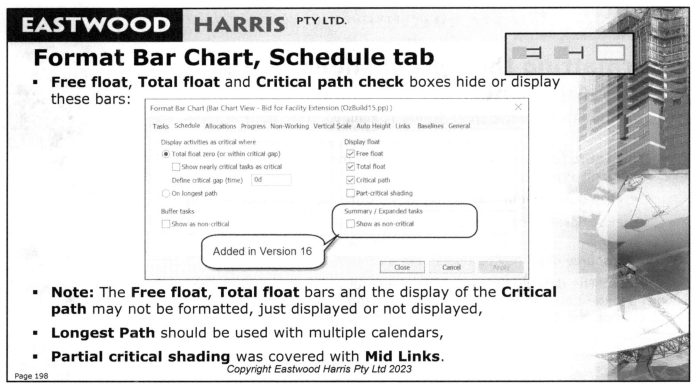

- **Note:** The **Free float**, **Total float** bars and the display of the **Critical path** may not be formatted, just displayed or not displayed,

- **Longest Path** should be used with multiple calendars,

- **Partial critical shading** was covered with **Mid Links**.

198

EASTWOOD HARRIS PTY LTD.

Link Categories

- **Link Categories** are created and formatted in the **Library Explorer**, and in turn assigned to Links,

- Links may be hidden from view by **Link Category** using the **Format Bar Chart** form, **Links** tab:

- Selected **Link Categories** may be ignored in schedule calculations from the **Reschedule**, **Options** form,

- **Note: Ignoring Link Categories** allows different build options in one schedule, such as East to West or West to East, or one or two crane options. This may save the requirement for two schedules when the tasks are the same for two options.

Reschedule

Options

Tasks with no links
- ○ Leave as drawn within constraints
- ○ Move if at project or chart bounds
- ● Move to ASAP/ALAP position

Tasks with only outgoing links
- ○ Leave as drawn within constraints
- ● Move to ASAP/ALAP position

Compatibility
- ☐ ALAP tasks have no free float
- ☐ Finish on or before flags are soft
- ☐ Summaries critical where content is critical
- ☑ Negative float applies to chain

Ignore link categories
- ☐ Default
- ☐ Important
- ☐ Normal
- ☐ Resource

Options
- ☑ Move part completed links
- ☐ Truncate float within chart boundaries
- ☐ Use delivery date as deadline
- ☐ Relink around completed tasks

Straighten progress line to period
- Progress entry period ⌄

- ☐ Only move forward to make straight
- ☐ Never move completed tasks

Compute
- ☐ Critical path drag

Format Bar Chart (Bar Chart View - OzBuild Bid (OzBuild.pp))

Tasks | Schedule | Allocations | Progress | Non-Working | Vertical Scale | Auto Height | Links | Baselines | General

Show
- ☑ Non-critical local links
- ☑ Critical local links
- ☑ Reflected links
- ☑ Non-critical half links
- ☑ Critical half links

Link categories to display
- ☑ Default
- ☑ Important
- ☑ Normal
- ☑ Resource

Driving links
- ☐ Hide non-driving links
- ☐ Distinguish non-driving links

- ☐ If critical, use critical display rather than category

Close | Cancel | Save

Page 199

199

EASTWOOD HARRIS PTY LTD.

Formatting the Spreadsheet using the Table function

- The formatting of the spreadsheet is achieved through the **Table** function,

- The **Table** formatting functions have far more options than P6 or Microsoft Project:

  - Each date column may be formatted with a different date format,

  - Most Baseline data fields may be viewed in columns,

  - Columns may be created to display the data for one resource only and the resource data may be updated in a column,

- **Note:** The default **Column title** does not indicate that it is displaying baseline data, so when a baseline column is displayed the user must change the **Column title** so it is clear that it is displaying baseline data.

Page 200

200

EASTWOOD HARRIS PTY LTD.

Adding Columns...

- To add a column right click on an existing column heading and select **Add Column**,

- You are now editing a **Table** of columns that may also be assigned to another **View**,

- Select a field from the menu; the categories are very different from P6 and Microsoft Project,

- A column is now added into the spreadsheet and the **Table Definition** form is opened,

- See next slide:

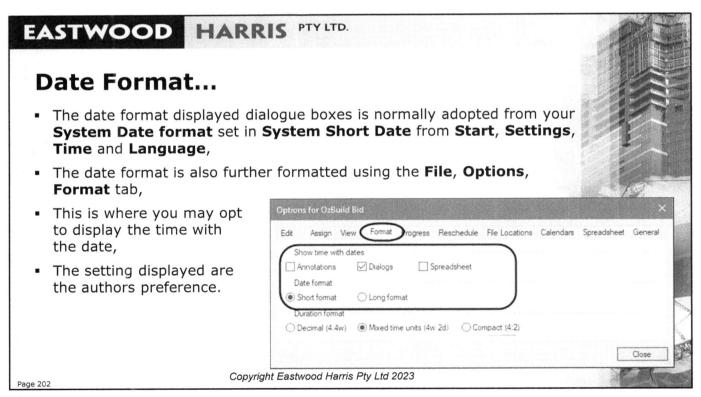

Page 201

201

EASTWOOD HARRIS PTY LTD.

Date Format...

- The date format displayed dialogue boxes is normally adopted from your **System Date format** set in **System Short Date** from **Start**, **Settings**, **Time** and **Language**,

- The date format is also further formatted using the **File**, **Options**, **Format** tab,

- This is where you may opt to display the time with the date,

- The setting displayed are the authors preference.

Page 202

202

EASTWOOD HARRIS PTY LTD.

Date Format

- Each date column may be formatted differently,
- To format a date column:
  - Right click on the appropriate column,
  - Select **Format Cells**, **Date/Time**,
  - Select the desired format from the drop-down list, or
  - Select Custom at the bottom of the list, "dd MMM yy" will give the format "12 Feb 21":

Page 203

203

EASTWOOD HARRIS PTY LTD.

Duration Format...

- It is initially formatted for a project in the **File**, **Options**, **Format** tab,
- The setting displayed is the authors preferred,
- Then the **Override time unit** in the **Table Definition Properties** form sets the next level of formatting, and
- Finally, the settings for each column may be overridden using the **Format Cells** form:

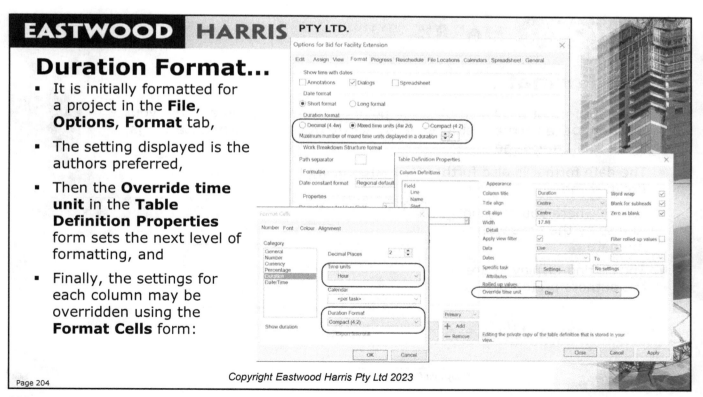

Page 204

204

EASTWOOD HARRIS PTY LTD.

Duration Format

- The Duration of Milestones may be displayed either:
  - As a number, e.g. 0 d, or
  - As a blank:

Table Definition Properties				
Column Definitions				
Field	Appearance			
Line	Column title	Duration	Word wrap	☑
Unique Task ID	Title align	Centre	Blank for subheads	☑
Name	Cell align	Centre	Zero as blank	☑
Start				
Duration	Width	17.88		
Finish	Detail			

Page 205

205

EASTWOOD HARRIS PTY LTD.

Saving the Table

- **Tables** of columns may be saved in the same way as Microsoft Project,
- **Tables** are created to display different data and reapplied at a later date,
- You may create a new table and edit it, or edit an existing table and then save as a new table,
- To create a new **Table**,
  - Select the **View** group, **Table**, **Save as**,
  - Give your **Table** a new name,
  - To switch between different tables select **View**, **Table** and select the table you require from the list of saved tables:

Page 206

206

EASTWOOD HARRIS PTY LTD.

Creating and Saving Views

- **Views** in Powerproject work in a similar way to Microsoft Project and similar to Layouts in P6

- A **View** holds the **Gantt Chart** and **Timescale** formatting and is assigned a **Group and Sort** and a **Table**, and may have a **Filter** assigned,

- After editing a **View**, say by assigning a different table, it may be saved by saving the project or a new View create using **Save View**,

- Each **View** may display project data with different formatting,

- To save the **View**:

  - On the **View** tab, **Views** group, **Save As**,

  - Give your **View** a name,

  - A **View Category** will show the new View sub menu,

- Applying another **View** will open the **View** in another window.

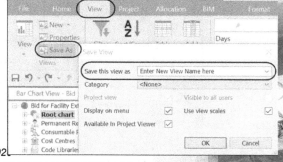

Page 207

207

EASTWOOD HARRIS PTY LTD.

Views, Tabs and Coloured Tabs

- As each new **View** is opened a new tab is displayed, and thus there will be multiple view for a project displayed,

- Clicking on the **X** on the tab will close a View,

- Closing the last **View** of a project will close a project,

- **Tabs** may be assigned a colour enabling simpler identification of projects when multiple projects are open as each project may have a different colour for their tabs,

- There is an article titled **What's New in Elecosoft (Asta) Powerproject Version 17** on www.eh.com.au which explains coloured tabs in detail.

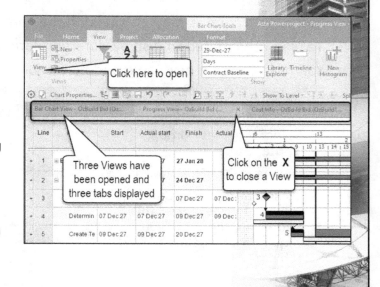

Page 208

208

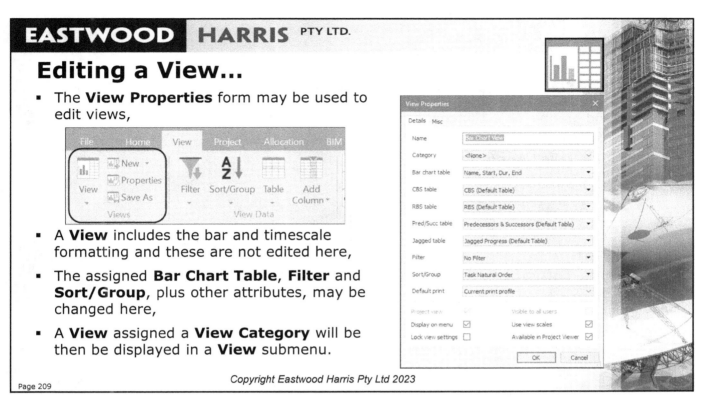

EASTWOOD HARRIS PTY LTD.

Editing a View...

- The **View Properties** form may be used to edit views,

- A **View** includes the bar and timescale formatting and these are not edited here,

- The assigned **Bar Chart Table**, **Filter** and **Sort/Group**, plus other attributes, may be changed here,

- A **View** assigned a **View Category** will be then be displayed in a **View** submenu.

Copyright Eastwood Harris Pty Ltd 2023

Page 209

209

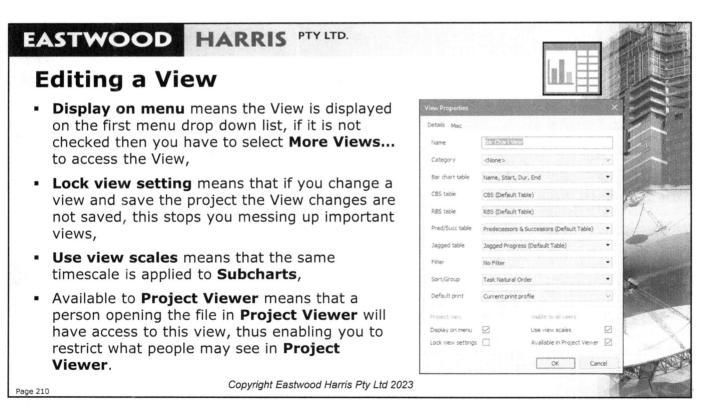

EASTWOOD HARRIS PTY LTD.

Editing a View

- **Display on menu** means the View is displayed on the first menu drop down list, if it is not checked then you have to select **More Views...** to access the View,

- **Lock view setting** means that if you change a view and save the project the View changes are not saved, this stops you messing up important views,

- **Use view scales** means that the same timescale is applied to **Subcharts**,

- Available to **Project Viewer** means that a person opening the file in **Project Viewer** will have access to this view, thus enabling you to restrict what people may see in **Project Viewer**.

Copyright Eastwood Harris Pty Ltd 2023

Page 210

210

EASTWOOD HARRIS PTY LTD.

Understanding Annotations

- Text and graphic objects may be placed on the Gantt Chart for reporting and presentation purposes,
- These are called **Annotations**,
- There are three types:
  - **Text Annotation**
  - **Object**
  - **Picture**
- Select the **Format** tab, **Annotations** to insert an **Annotation**.

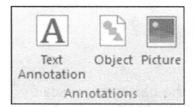

Page 211

211

EASTWOOD HARRIS PTY LTD.

Creating a Text Annotation...

- To add a **Text Annotation** select **Format**, **Annotations**, **Text Annotation**,
- Place the cursor on the Gantt chart until the letter **T** is displayed, this will put the Annotation on the Gantt Chart,
- To attach the Annotation to a bar move the mouse around the bar and select the anchor point, the mouse shapes are self explanatory,
- Draw a box with the mouse,
- Add your text, or
- You may also right click to add a **Powerproject field** or **formulae** from the drop down box.

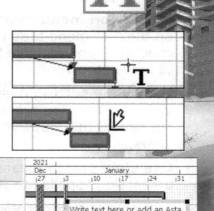

Page 212

212

EASTWOOD HARRIS PTY LTD.

Creating a Text Annotation

- To format the text click out and then right click on the Annotation and select **Properties** to open the **Text Annotation Properties** form:

- **Make Auto Annotation** will apply the Annotation to all bars, and

- The **Filter** will allow the selection of bars that the Annotation is applied.

Text Annotation Properties

General Scaling

Drawing
Background colour:

☑ Show border

Font...

Filter
<None>

☐ Make Auto Annotation

Drawing Layer
◉ Foreground
○ Background
○ Back

Category
Text on Plan

Properties   New...

(Auto annotations may not be made where the annotation is attached to a baseline object, or where the view has not been saved.)

Close

EASTWOOD HARRIS PTY LTD.

Creating an Object Annotation

- Click the **Object** annotation toolbar button or go to **Insert**, **Object**,

- Place the cursor on the Gantt Chart,

- Draw a box,

- The **Insert Object** form will open allowing linking to an Object:

Insert Object

Object Type:
◉ Create New
○ Create from File

Adobe Acrobat Document
Adobe Photoshop Image
Microsoft Excel 97-2003 Worksheet
Microsoft Excel Binary Worksheet
Microsoft Excel Chart
Microsoft Excel Macro-Enabled Work
Microsoft Excel Worksheet
Microsoft Graph Chart

OK
Cancel

☐ Display As Icon

Result
Inserts a new Adobe Acrobat Document object into your document.

EASTWOOD HARRIS PTY LTD.

Picture Annotation

- Select **Format**, **Annotations**, **Picture** to add a graphic to the Gantt Chart,

- Browse and add a graphic,

- To re-size the picture click on it and use the resizing arrows, or use the hand to reposition a picture:

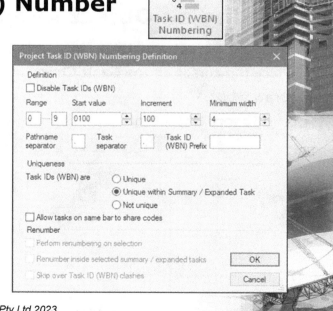

Page 215

215

EASTWOOD HARRIS PTY LTD.

Project Task ID or (WBN) Number Definition

- You may number your tasks with a hierarchal numbering system called **Task ID (WBN)** numbering,

- The **Project, Properties, Project Task ID or (WBN) Number Definition** form is used to define or renumber the structure,

- It is probably better to use the newer WBS function if you wish to show a Hierarchical WBS structure:

Task ID (WBN) Numbering

Project Task ID (WBN) Numbering Definition

Definition
☐ Disable Task IDs (WBN)

Range	Start value	Increment	Minimum width
0 — 9	0100	100	4

Pathname separator: [.]   Task separator: [.]   Task ID (WBN) Prefix: [ ]

Uniqueness
Task IDs (WBN) are
○ Unique
◉ Unique within Summary / Expanded Task
○ Not unique

☐ Allow tasks on same bar to share codes

Renumber
☐ Perform renumbering on selection
☐ Renumber inside selected summary / expanded tasks
☐ Skip over Task ID (WBN) clashes

[OK]   [Cancel]

Page 216

216

EASTWOOD HARRIS PTY LTD.

Unique Task ID Numbering

- A **Unique Task ID** may be assigned in a similar method to Oracle Primavera P6 Activity ID using the **Unique Task ID Numbering** function,

- This is best set up before you add tasks,

- Then they may be renumbered using the **Unique Task ID Numbering** function:

217

EASTWOOD HARRIS PTY LTD.

Displaying Task ID or (WBN) or Unique Task IDs

- Display the following columns to display the Task ID (WBN) codes:
  - **Unique task ID**
  - **Task ID (WBN)** and
  - **Task ID (WBN) Pathname:**

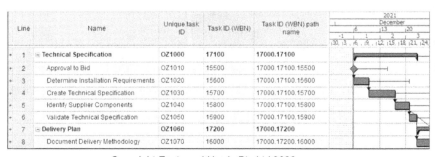

Line	Name	Unique task ID	Task ID (WBN)	Task ID (WBN) path name
1	⊟ Technical Specification	OZ1000	17100	17000.17100
2	Approval to Bid	OZ1010	15500	17000.17100.15500
3	Determine Installation Requirements	OZ1020	15600	17000.17100.15600
4	Create Technical Specification	OZ1030	15700	17000.17100.15700
5	Identify Supplier Components	OZ1040	15800	17000.17100.15800
6	Validate Technical Specification	OZ1050	15900	17000.17100.15900
7	⊟ Delivery Plan	OZ1060	17200	17000.17200
8	Document Delivery Methodology	OZ1070	16000	17000.17200.16000

218

EASTWOOD HARRIS PTY LTD.

Timeline View

There is now a Microsoft Project style **Timeline View**:

- To hide or display the **Timeline View** select **View**, **Show**, **Timeline**, or

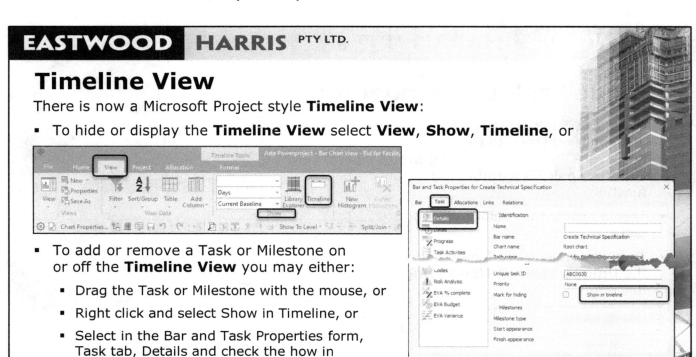

- To add or remove a Task or Milestone on or off the **Timeline View** you may either:

  - Drag the Task or Milestone with the mouse, or

  - Right click and select Show in Timeline, or

  - Select in the Bar and Task Properties form, Task tab, Details and check the how in Timeline check box:

EASTWOOD HARRIS PTY LTD.

Timeline View

In version 17 a task may be displayed in one of two ways by right clicking in the **Timeline**, either as a:

- **Bar** with a bar showing the task duration, or

- **Callout** where the task name and other information is displayed as a callout and is not scaled to the to the start and finish like a bar,

- Click into the **Timeline** menu to display the **Timeline** toolbar.

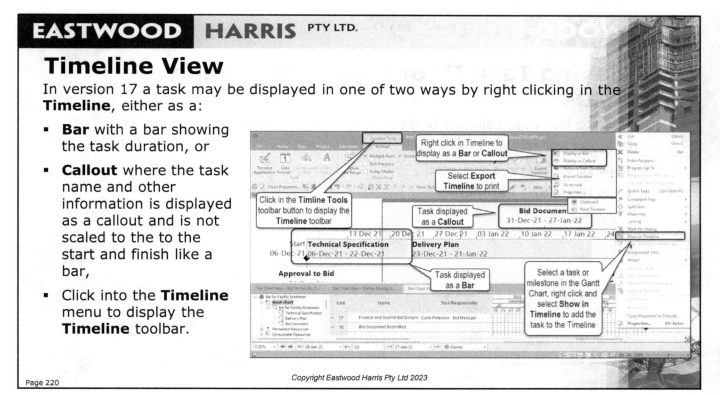

EASTWOOD HARRIS PTY LTD.

Timeline View

- To print the Timeline one has to use the **Export Timeline** and this is found by:
  - By right clicking in the Timeline, or
  - Using the **Export Timeline** command found on the **Timeline** toolbar.
- Security to the Timeline may be controlled from the **Library Explorer**, **Security Group Properties**:

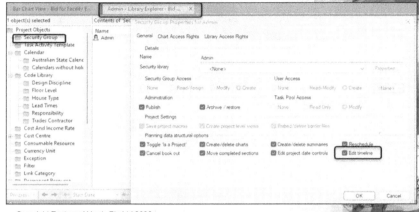

Page 221

221

EASTWOOD HARRIS PTY LTD.

9 - FORMATTING THE DISPLAY - SUMMARY

We have covered in this module formatting:

- The Date Zone, Gridlines, Vertical Shading and Multiple Date Zones,
- Hiding non-working time,
- Formatting bars and Links,
- Adding Notes,
- Link Categories,
- Columns, Date and Durations,
- Tables and Views,
- Adding Annotations,
- Task Numbering,
- Timeline View.

Page 222

222

EASTWOOD HARRIS PTY LTD.

Workshop 9 - Formatting the Bar Chart

- We will make some changes to the View to practise some of the skills covered in this module.

223

EASTWOOD HARRIS PTY LTD.

10 - CODE LIBRARIES

In this module we will cover:

- Creating Code Libraries
- Assigning Codes to Tasks
- Selecting which Code is displayed on task bars
- Introduction to filters.

224

EASTWOOD HARRIS PTY LTD.

Understanding Code Libraries

- Code Libraries in Powerproject are similar to Activity Codes in P6 and Outline Codes in Microsoft Project, but are more powerful than either of the P6 and Microsoft Project functions:
  - Tasks may be coloured by Code (like P6 Visualizer) and
  - Tasks may be assigned multiple Codes, unlike P6 or Microsoft Project,
  - **Note:** Assigning multiple codes to a task is useful for situations such as when 3 building floor codes may be assigned to a column task that spans three floors,
- Codes are created in the **Library Explorer**,
- Codes may be assigned in a number of ways but typically by dragging from the **Project View**,
- Codes may also be assigned from columns or from the **Bar & Task Properties** view or form,
- Powerproject Version 16 allows multiple code colouring of tasks with restrictions.

Page 225   *Copyright Eastwood Harris Pty Ltd 2023*

225

EASTWOOD HARRIS PTY LTD.

Creating a New Code Library

- This example demonstrates the creation of a Responsibility Code Library,
  - Click the **Library Explorer** toolbar button,
  - Click on the **Code Library** folder in the left window of **Library Explorer**:
  - Right click in a blank part of the screen and select **New Code Library**,

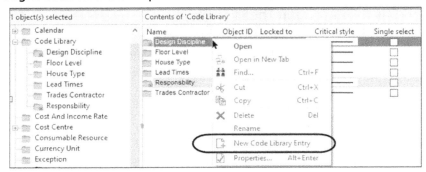

  - The picture above shows a new Code titled **Responsibility**.

Page 226   *Copyright Eastwood Harris Pty Ltd 2023*

226

Creating New Codes

- Double click on the code folder to open it,

- Right click in the right hand pane and choose **New Code Library Entry**,

- Double click on the new entry and complete the form,

- The **Sort Order** column allows an alternative sort order for the Code display in both the **Project View** and on the screen,

- Unless you require your codes to always be sorted alphabetically you should use the **Sort order** option.

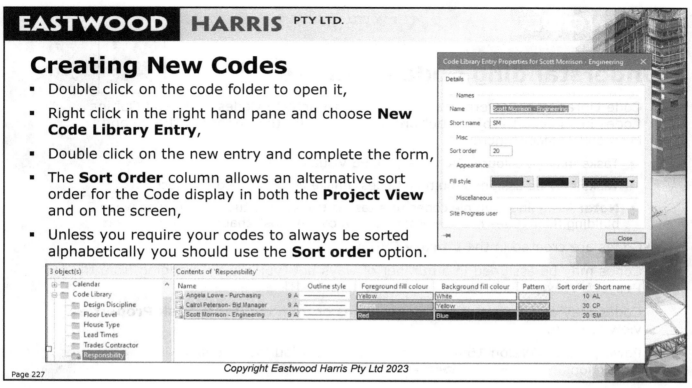

Copyright Eastwood Harris Pty Ltd 2023

Page 227

227

Assigning codes to tasks

- The **File**, **Options**, **View** tab **Sort/group entries by:** sets the sort order of codes in both **Project View** and the on screen sort order,

- Unchecking the **Show code library appearance hides** the bar formatting in the **Project View**,

- Assigning codes to tasks may be achieved using:

  - Dragging from the **Project View**,

  - The **Bar and Task Properties** view,

  - The **Bar and Task Properties** form,

  - Displaying the appropriate columns,

  - Applying a table with the appropriate columns.

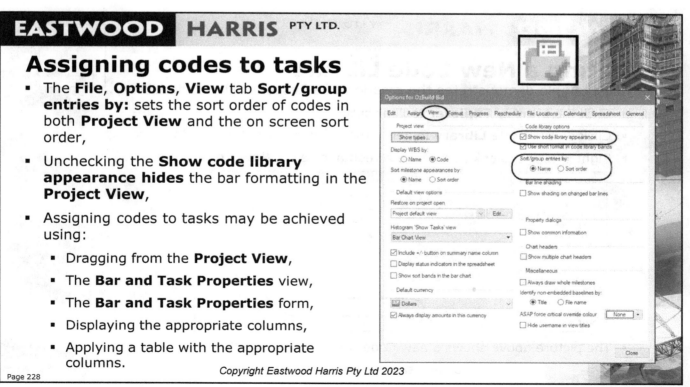

Copyright Eastwood Harris Pty Ltd 2023

Page 228

228

EASTWOOD HARRIS PTY LTD.

Assigning a Code to a Single Task

- To assign a code to a single task,
  - Place the cursor on the code in the **Project View**,
  - Left click and drag to the task bar in the Gantt Chart,
  - You may receive the following message,

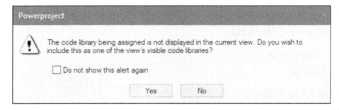

Powerproject

⚠ The code library being assigned is not displayed in the current view. Do you wish to include this as one of the view's visible code libraries?

☐ Do not show this alert again

Yes   No

  - Click **Yes** to apply the new **Code Library** formatting to all the task bars.

Page 229

229

EASTWOOD HARRIS PTY LTD.

Assigning a Code to a Multiple Tasks

- To assign a code to a multiple tasks,
  - Select multiple task bars in the Gantt Chart or Line No by Crtl clicking,
  - Place the cursor on the code in the **Project View**,
  - Left click and drag the Code Value on to one of the task bars in the Gantt Chart,
  - You may receive the following message,

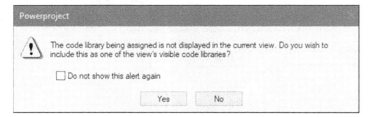

Powerproject

⚠ The code library being assigned is not displayed in the current view. Do you wish to include this as one of the view's visible code libraries?

☐ Do not show this alert again

Yes   No

  - Click **Yes** to apply the new Code Library colour to all the task bars.

Page 230

230

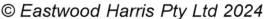
115

EASTWOOD HARRIS PTY LTD.

Selecting which code is displayed on task bars

- When one **Code Library** is to be used to format the tasks,

- From the **Project View**,

  - Select the **Code Library** :

  - Right Click on the Code Library heading and select **Display Library**,

  - The red tick identifies the code library used to colour tasks,

- Version 14 and earlier only allowed one **Code Library** to be displayed on tasks,

- In Version 15 if any other Code Libraries have a red tick this needs to be removed using the same process so only one Code Library has a red tick.

OzBuild Bid
- Root chart
- Permanent Reso
- Consumable Res
- Cost Centres
- Code Libraries
  - Build Stages
  - Design Discip
  - Floor Level
  - House Type
  - Lead Times
  - Responsibilit
  - Trades Cont
- Calendars
  - Australian State Calendars

Menu:
- Open Code Breakdown Structure
- Delete — Del
- Rename
- New Code Library Entry
- Display Library
- Multiple Display Libraries...
- Open in New Tab
- Expand
- Contract
- Properties... — Alt+Enter

Page 231

231

EASTWOOD HARRIS PTY LTD.

Open Code Breakdown Structure Command

To quickly view your tasks under their Codes:

- Right click on the **Code Library** heading and

- Select **Open Code Breakdown Structure**:

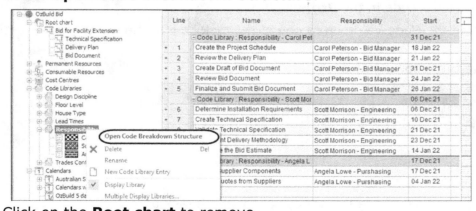

	Line	Name	Responsibility	Start	
		- Code Library : Responsibility - Carol Pet		31 Dec 21	
	1	Create the Project Schedule	Carol Peterson - Bid Manager	18 Jan 22	
	2	Review the Delivery Plan	Carol Peterson - Bid Manager	21 Jan 22	
	3	Create Draft of Bid Document	Carol Peterson - Bid Manager	31 Dec 21	
	4	Review Bid Document	Carol Peterson - Bid Manager	24 Jan 22	
	5	Finalize and Submit Bid Document	Carol Peterson - Bid Manager	26 Jan 22	
		- Code Library : Responsibility - Scott Mor		06 Dec 21	
	6	Determine Installation Requirements	Scott Morrison - Engineering	06 Dec 21	
	7	Create Technical Specification	Scott Morrison - Engineering	10 Dec 21	
		Validate Technical Specification	Scott Morrison - Engineering	21 Dec 21	
		nt Delivery Methodology	Scott Morrison - Engineering	23 Dec 21	
		the Bid Estimate	Scott Morrison - Engineering	14 Jan 22	
		rary : Responsibility - Angela L		17 Dec 21	
		upplier Components	Angela Lowe - Purshasing	17 Dec 21	
		uotes from Suppliers	Angela Lowe - Purshasing	04 Jan 22	

- Click on the **Root chart** to remove.

Page 232

232

EASTWOOD HARRIS PTY LTD.

Multiple Display Libraries

- A new function in Powerproject Version 15 allows the formatting of bars to be read from multiple Codes Libraries using the **Multiple Display Libraries** option,

- When more than one Code Library has been assigned to a task:

  - Only one Code Library will be displayed on the bar,

  - The colouring from the Code highest in the list in the **Multiple Display Libraries** form is displayed on the bar.

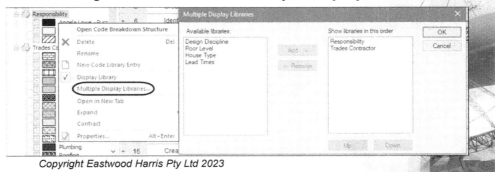

233

EASTWOOD HARRIS PTY LTD.

Introduction to filters...

- Now that the project is coded, filters may be used to show only the tasks with a certain code,

- To filter on a code:

  - Select the **View** tab, **View Data** group, **Filter**, and

  - Select a **Code Based** filter that may be named differently to the picture:

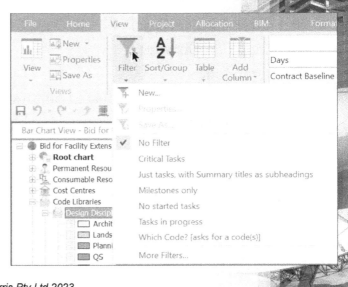

234

Introduction to filters

- Click on the + against the required code to display the available codes,

- Check the required values,

- Click on **Finish** to run the filter,

- Select **View**, **Filter**, **No Filter** to remove the filter.

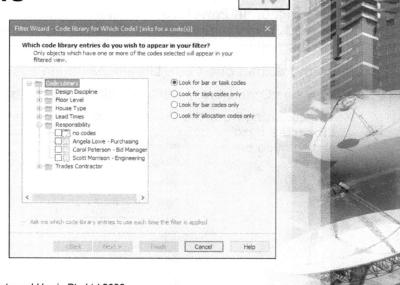

10 - CODE LIBRARIES - SUMMARY

In this module we covered:

- Creating Code Libraries

- Assigning Codes to Tasks

- Selecting which code is displayed on task bars

- Introduction to filters.

EASTWOOD HARRIS PTY LTD.

Workshop 10 – Code Libraries

- We want to issue reports for comment by management by assigning responsibility to the activities, and
- Then applying filters for each responsible person.

237

EASTWOOD HARRIS PTY LTD.

11 - FILTERS

In this module we will cover:

- Filtering using the Root Chart
- Understanding Filters
- Applying a Filter
- Creating a New Filter.

238

EASTWOOD HARRIS PTY LTD.

Filtering using the Root Chart

- Often it is simpler to reduce the number of tasks in view by selecting the appropriate nodes in the **Root Chart**,

- This may be only completed when **Summary Tasks** are used and not when tasks are grouped by WBS or Code,

- The picture below shows only the tasks under the two selected **Summary Tasks**:

Page 239

Copyright Eastwood Harris Pty Ltd 2023

239

EASTWOOD HARRIS PTY LTD.

Understanding Filters

- Powerproject has an ability to display tasks that meet specific criteria using filters,

- Powerproject defaults to displaying all tasks,

- Templates may include a number of predefined filters that you may use or edit and you may also create one or more of your own,

- Interactive filters may be created and may be customised when applied. For example a filter may be created to select a code value and the value is selected from a list when the filter applied. This works in a similar way to a Microsoft Interactive Filter,

- The **Filter Wizard** designed to create filters but is difficult to use,

- The simplest way to create a new filter is to copy an existing filter with similar parameters and edit it.

Page 240

Copyright Eastwood Harris Pty Ltd 2023

240

Understanding Filters

- Filters may be viewed in the filter menu or **Library Explorer**,
- Filters may be assigned a **Filter Category** and then they are displayed in a **Filter** submenu,
- Filters may also be hidden from all menus and only displayed in the **More Filter Menu** when **Display** on menu is not checked,
- These attributes may be seen in the **Library Explorer**:

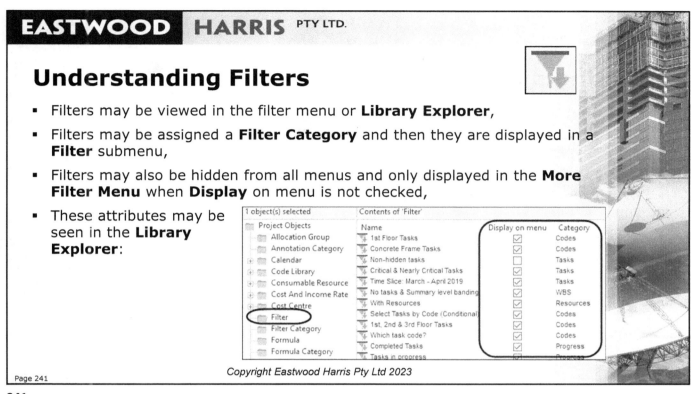

Copyright Eastwood Harris Pty Ltd 2023

Page 241

241

Applying an Existing Filter

- Filters are displayed in the main **Filter Menu** when they are not assigned a **Filter Category** or
- Displayed in a **Submenu** when assigned a **Filter Category**:

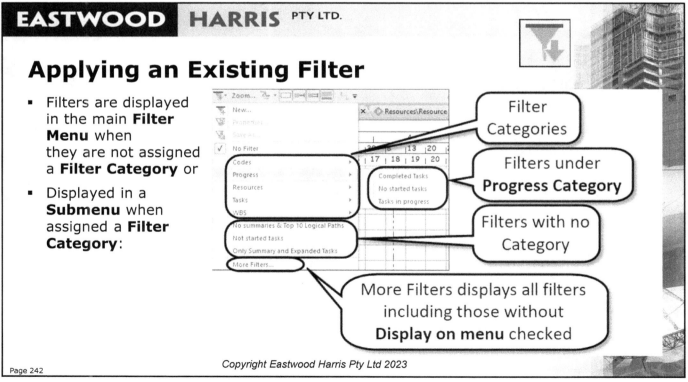

Copyright Eastwood Harris Pty Ltd 2023

Page 242

242

EASTWOOD HARRIS PTY LTD.

Creating a New Filter

- There are two ways of creating a new filter:
  - Select **View**, **Filter**, **New:** and use the **Filter Wizard** to create a new filter, or
  - **Copy** an existing one using the **Save As** function,
- The **Filter Wizard** is complex and has many dialogue boxes that are not simple to master,
- Often it is simpler to copy an existing filter that is similar to the one you require and edit it,
- **Note:** You may also open another project and copy and paste a filter from another project using **Library Explorer**.

Page 243

243

EASTWOOD HARRIS PTY LTD.

Creating a New Filter using the Filter Wizard...

To create a new filter:

- Select **View**, **Filter**, **New**,
- Assign the filter a **Name**,
- To add the filter to the **Menu** select **Display on menu**,
- Assign a **Category** if required,
- Multiple **Criteria** are allowed and select **Insert** to insert a second Criteria line,
- Complete the **Criteria logic** and **Filter options**,
- **Subheading properties** allows a hierarchy of summary tasks to be concatenated on one line,
- Select **Edit** to edit the selected criteria filter.

Page 244

244

Creating a New Filter using the Filter Wizard...

- Select **Edit** to edit the filter **Conditions** and select **Next**,
- Depending on the type of filter the forms are different,
- Select the specific data to filter on and click **Back** or **Next**:

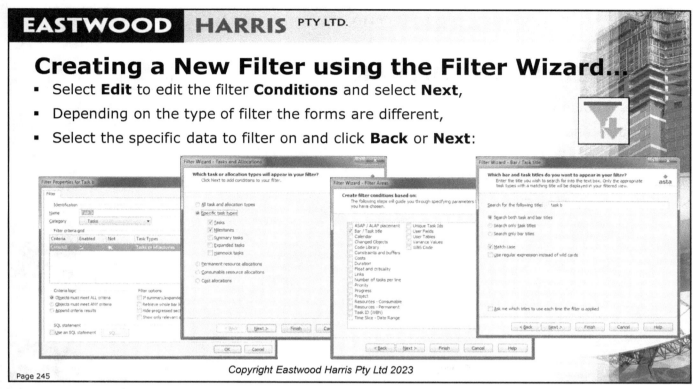

Page 245
Copyright Eastwood Harris Pty Ltd 2023

245

Creating a New Filter using the Filter Wizard

- Check the data at the **Summary** dialogue box and select **Finish**,
- **Filters** may be run by selecting the **Filter** icon from the tool bar.

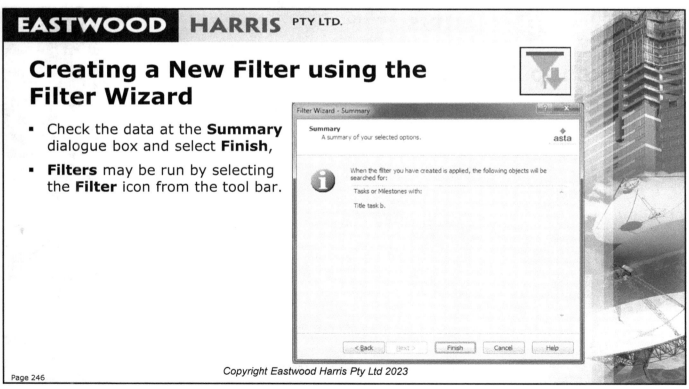

Page 246
Copyright Eastwood Harris Pty Ltd 2023

246

EASTWOOD HARRIS PTY LTD.

11 – FILTERS - SUMMARY

In this module we covered:

- Understanding Filters
- Applying a Filter
- Filtering using the Root Chart
- Creating a New Filter.

Page 247

247

EASTWOOD HARRIS PTY LTD.

Workshop 11 - Filters

- In this workshop we will apply some existing filters.

Page 248

248

EASTWOOD HARRIS PTY LTD.

12 – ORGANISING TASKS USING SORT AND GROUP

- Powerproject may **Sort and Group** tasks on **Codes** and other project parameters in the same way as P6 or Microsoft Project,

- This function is used to group tasks by Codes such as trade, floor, area, responsibility, contractor etc, or by other parameters such as the Task Calendar or Float,

- This module will show you how to create and apply a **Sort and Group**,

- The **Sort/Group Properties** form is used to create new **Sort and Group** has may options and takes a little time to understand,

- A **Sort and Group** is applied to and save with a **View**,

- Often the simplest way to create a new **Sort and Group** is to copy an existing one with similar parameters and edit it.

Page 249

249

EASTWOOD HARRIS PTY LTD.

Creating a Sort and Group...

The **Sort and Group** to be demonstrated in this module will use the Responsibility Code library,

- Select **View**, **Sort/Group**,

- Select **New...**, to open the **Sort/Group Properties** form,

- Assign a name for the sort, e.g. **By Responsibility**,

- Select a **Category** if required,

- Check **Display on menu** if you want the **Group/Sort** displayed in the menu.

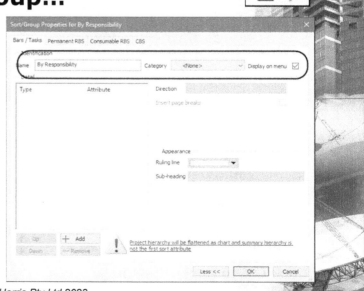

Page 250

250

Creating a Sort and Group...

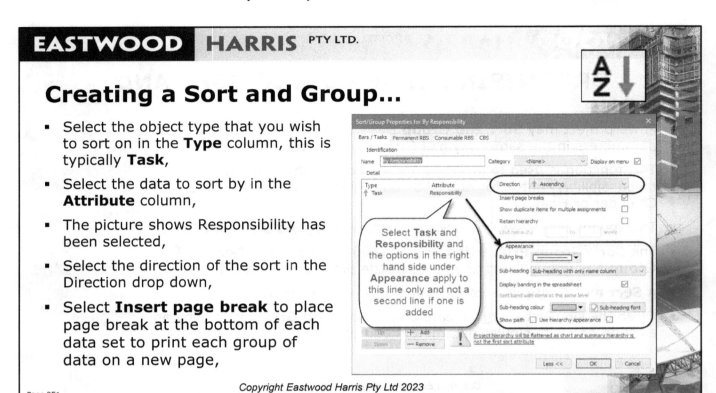

- Select the object type that you wish to sort on in the **Type** column, this is typically **Task**,
- Select the data to sort by in the **Attribute** column,
- The picture shows Responsibility has been selected,
- Select the direction of the sort in the Direction drop down,
- Select **Insert page break** to place page break at the bottom of each data set to print each group of data on a new page,

Copyright Eastwood Harris Pty Ltd 2023

Page 251

251

Creating a Sort and Group...

Check the other options as required,

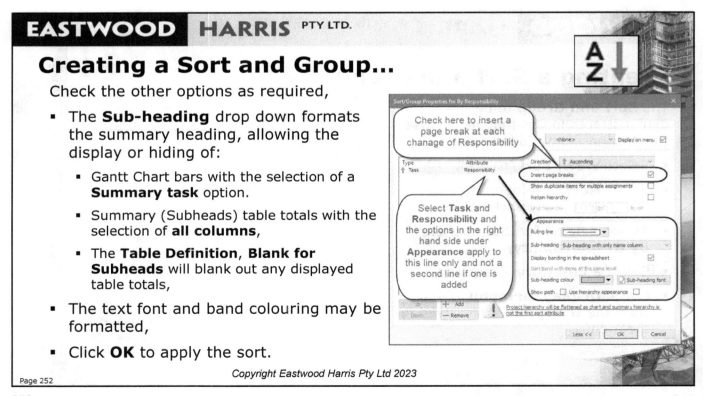

- The **Sub-heading** drop down formats the summary heading, allowing the display or hiding of:
  - Gantt Chart bars with the selection of a **Summary task** option.
  - Summary (Subheads) table totals with the selection of **all columns**,
  - The **Table Definition**, **Blank for Subheads** will blank out any displayed table totals,
- The text font and band colouring may be formatted,
- Click **OK** to apply the sort.

Copyright Eastwood Harris Pty Ltd 2023

Page 252

252

EASTWOOD HARRIS PTY LTD.

Creating a Sort and Group...

- The simple **Group and Sort** demonstrated will give the result as per below,
- The dark dotted horizontal lines are page break lines:

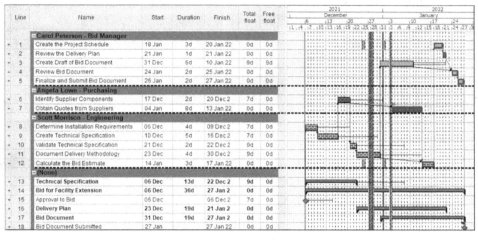

Page 253

253

EASTWOOD HARRIS PTY LTD.

Creating a Sort and Group...

- If you want the activities ordered in a specific way you may add a second line to sort the tasks,
- The picture below displays the task sorted alphabetically:

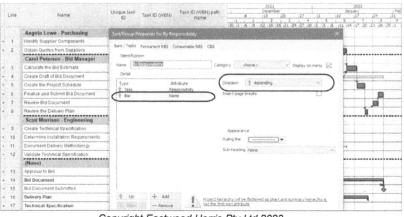

Page 254

254

Creating a Sort and Group

- Tasks may be grouped by a second band,
- The picture below displays the task Grouped by Responsibility and Calendar:

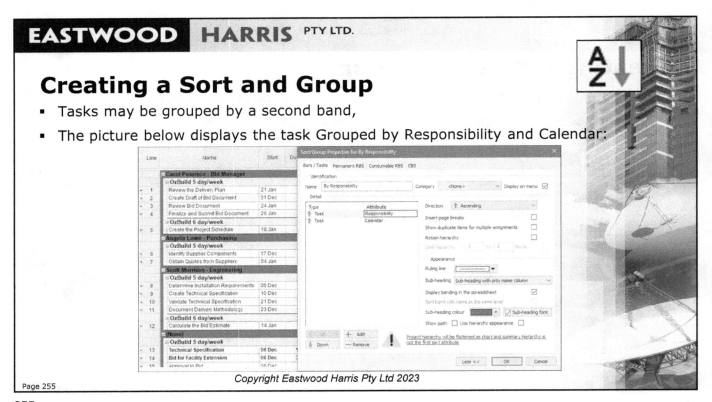

Creating a Sort and Group

- **Project Hierarchy** is by default the first line and when this is removed then the **Task-per-line function** is disabled,
- When **Project Hierarchy** is left as the first line then activities are first Grouped by the Summary Tasks first.

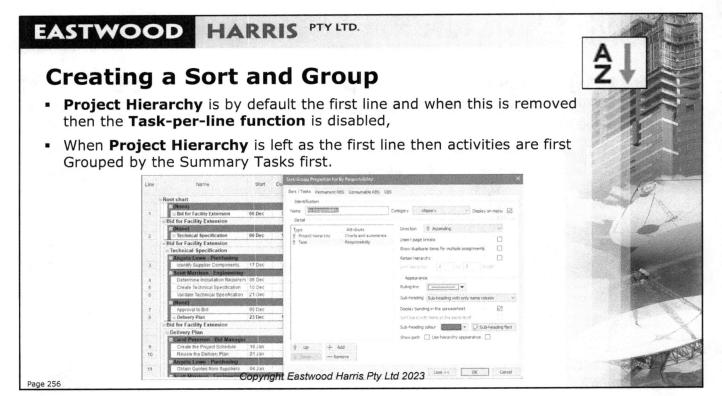

Removing a Group and Sort

- Selecting **Natural Order** from the **Group/Sort** menu will remove all Grouping and Sorting,

- This option will then sort the tasks by the outlined summary tasks,

- Selecting **Natural Order** is the same as having a **Group/Sort** by **Project Hierarchy** only.

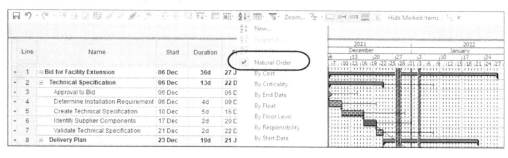

Page 257

257

EASTWOOD HARRIS PTY LTD.

12 – ORGANISING TASKS USING SORT AND GROUP - SUMMARY

In this module we have covered how to:

- Create and apply a **Sort and Group** and

- Remove a **Sort and Group**.

Page 258

258

EASTWOOD HARRIS PTY LTD.

Workshop 12 - Organizing Tasks using Sort and Group

- You will create a **Sort and Group** to group the tasks by Responsibility.

Page 259

259

EASTWOOD HARRIS PTY LTD.

13 - PRINTING & REPORTS

There are some tools available to output your schedule to a printer and produce reports:

- The **Printing** function prints the data displayed in the current View,

- You may wish to create views that are used just for printing, so you do not mess them up while creating and updating your program,

- **Powerdraw** is used to edit your **Border files** for formatting your printout borders, this enables borders to be created so they are in proportion to your paper,

- The **Reporting** function prints reports or export reports to Excel, which are independent of the current **View**,

- Powerproject supplies a number of predefined reports that may be tailored to suit your own requirements.

Page 260

260

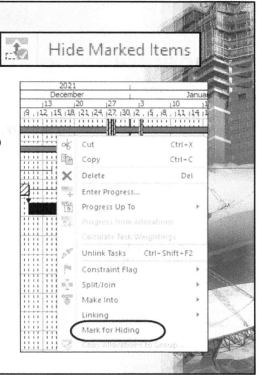

EASTWOOD HARRIS PTY LTD.

Hiding Tasks before Printing...

- Sometimes you may wish to temporarily hide some tasks before printing,

- This is similar to filtering but the tasks do not have to meet a criteria,

- In order to hide specific tasks, you must first mark them for hiding, and then hide them:

  - Select one or more the task bars in the Gantt Chart,

  - Right click and select **Mark For Hiding** from the menu that appears or click on the Quick Access Toolbar button after it has been added,

  - Once you have marked items you may hide or display them from view at any time by clicking the **Hide Marked Items** button when added to a toolbar.

Copyright Eastwood Harris Pty Ltd 2023

Page 261

261

EASTWOOD HARRIS PTY LTD.

Hiding Tasks before Printing

- To show Hidden tasks:

  - When tasks are hidden, the **Hide Marked Items** toolbar button changes to have a highlighted background,

  - The **Hide Marked Items** toolbar button may be clicked at any time to restore the hidden tasks,

- To unmark the tasks so they are not hidden in future:

  - Select the task,

  - Right click in the Gantt Chart and select **Mark for Hiding** again to unmark the tasks,

- The **Mark for hiding** column may be displayed to identify which tasks are marked and to mark tasks.

Copyright Eastwood Harris Pty Ltd 2023

Page 262

262

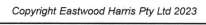

EASTWOOD HARRIS PTY LTD.

Understanding Powerdraw and Border Files

- A **Border** file is a separate file that is edited with **Powerdraw**,
- **Powerdraw** is started separately to Powerproject either from the **Start Menu** or using the **Print, Print Options, Details, Edit** icon,
- This function allows:
  - Scaling of the border to suit different paper sizes and
  - Creation of multiple borders with different fields that are read from the Powerproject file and may be applied to multiple projects,
- Powerproject is supplied with a set of Boarder files that you may use or edit.

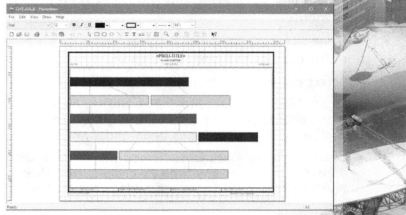

Page 263

263

EASTWOOD HARRIS PTY LTD.

Printing the Project

- Select **File, Print** or select the **Print** button,
- **Print Now** will print the project with the existing options,
- **Print Options** allows you to format the printout,
- **Full Preview** uses the whole screen for preview and access to formatting commands through a toolbar.

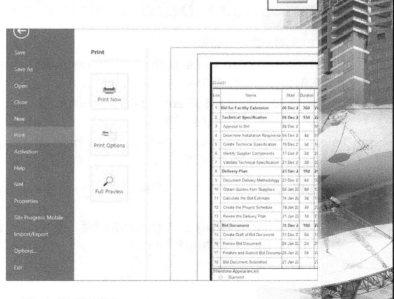

Page 264

264

EASTWOOD HARRIS PTY LTD.

Print Options, Output - Understanding Clipboard and Picture File

- **Printer** is self explanatory,
- **Clipboard** is where Powerproject takes a 'snap shot' of your project and then you may paste it into another program from the Clipboard,
- **Picture File** is similar to the clipboard option:
  - But instead of storing it in the computers memory it writes it as a picture file (JPEG extension),
  - Thus, you may either email it or insert it as a picture object in another application such as Word, PowerPoint, Excel or Outlook.

Page 265

Copyright Eastwood Harris Pty Ltd 2023

265

EASTWOOD HARRIS PTY LTD.

Print Options, Details

- Select **Browse...** from the **Details** tab and select your border file,
- Then select the orientation and page size,
- **Date Range**,
- **Embed** saves the border as part of the project file,
- The current print options may be saved as a **Print profile** and then applied to other projects.

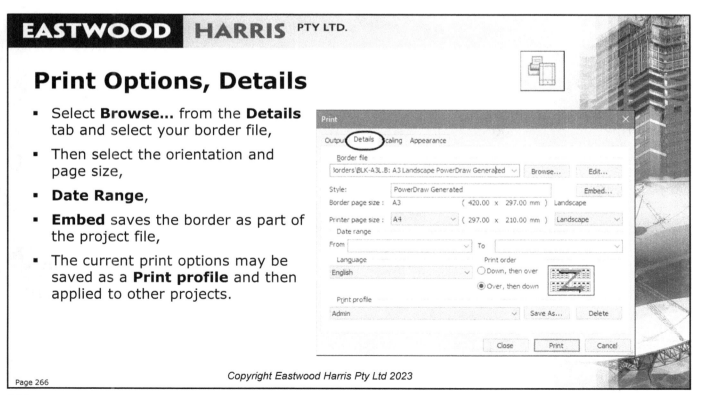

Page 266

Copyright Eastwood Harris Pty Ltd 2023

266

Print Options, Scaling

- The **Scaling** tab option allows control over the scaling of the horizontal and vertical scales of the table and Gantt Chart,

- This form is very busy and initially difficult to understand, but is written in plain English,

- To use **Page Breaks** you must select:

    - **One border page** and

    - Select options below **One border page** that allow the **Use defined page breaks check box** to be highlighted, such as **True size** or **Fit lines per page**.

Page 267

Copyright Eastwood Harris Pty Ltd 2023

267

Print Options, Appearance

- This form allows further formatting of the output:

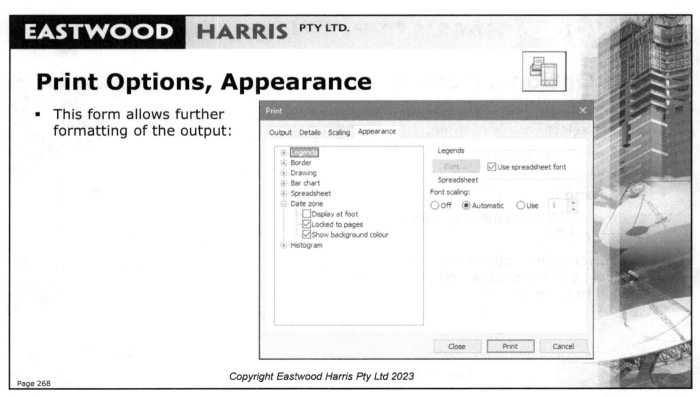

Page 268

Copyright Eastwood Harris Pty Ltd 2023

268

134

EASTWOOD HARRIS PTY LTD.

Page Breaks

- Powerproject allows two different types of page breaks,

    - First are the **Defined Page Breaks** are created by right clicking one or more bars where you want the page break to be set, right clicking and selecting Page Break,

    - **Defined Page Breaks** are removed by repeating the process, and

    - Second are the **Page Breaks** set in the **Sort and Group** form.

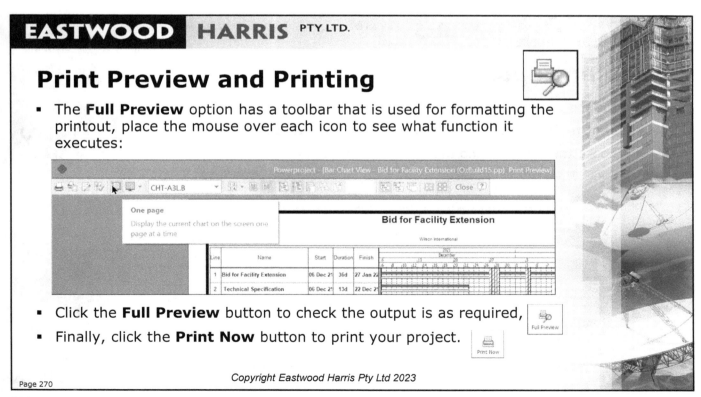

269

EASTWOOD HARRIS PTY LTD.

Print Preview and Printing

- The **Full Preview** option has a toolbar that is used for formatting the printout, place the mouse over each icon to see what function it executes:

- Click the **Full Preview** button to check the output is as required,

- Finally, click the **Print Now** button to print your project.

270

Reports

EASTWOOD HARRIS PTY LTD.

- Powerproject has many inbuilt tabular reports that may be exported in many formats,
- These are typically exported in to Excel for formatting and presentation purposes.

Page 271

271

EASTWOOD HARRIS PTY LTD.

Tabular Reports

- To produce a tabular report:
    - Select the **Project**, **Data**, **Reports** to open the **Reports** menu,
    - Choose the category and the report you wish to run:

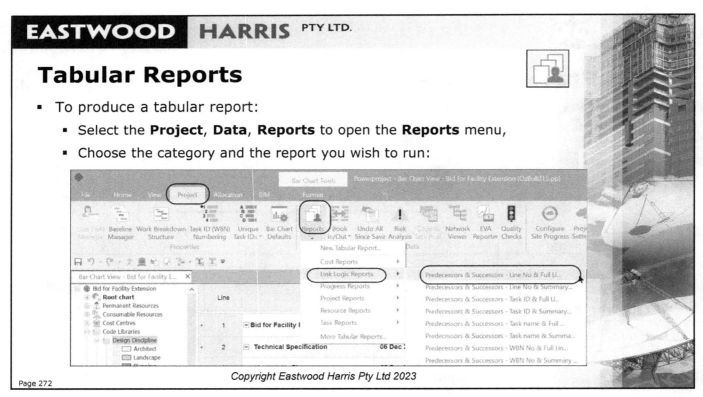

Page 272

272

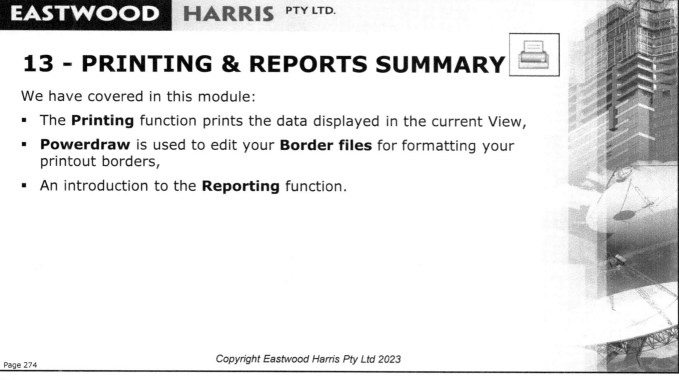

EASTWOOD HARRIS PTY LTD.

Tabular Reports...

- Tabular Reports are specified in the **Report Properties** form which is opened from the **Reports, More Tabular Reports...**, then select the report and click on **Properties**,

- This form also specifies where the report is run in the **Output** tab.

EASTWOOD HARRIS PTY LTD.

13 - PRINTING & REPORTS SUMMARY

We have covered in this module:

- The **Printing** function prints the data displayed in the current View,

- **Powerdraw** is used to edit your **Border files** for formatting your printout borders,

- An introduction to the **Reporting** function.

EASTWOOD HARRIS PTY LTD.

Workshop 13 - Printing

- You will print your project.

Page 275

275

EASTWOOD HARRIS PTY LTD.

14 – BASELINES

- A Baseline is a software function used to record the project status at a particular point in time allowing comparison of project progress at different stages,

- Baselines may be used to:
  - Compare progress with an agreed contract plan, or
  - Compare one periods' progress with another, in order to evaluate slippage etc., or
  - For claims analysis, with the Baseline recording the status before a delay or acceleration is applied to the Live schedule,

- A Baseline may record all or some activities and includes all task data such as bars, tasks, links, resource/cost allocations, libraries, histograms and annotations,

- Unlike P6, part projects in Powerproject may be baselined,

- Microsoft Project does not Baseline logic, constraints or the critical path.

Page 276

276

EASTWOOD HARRIS PTY LTD.

Powerproject Version 15 Baseline functionality changes

- In earlier versions of Powerproject a baseline was saved as a separate file with a *.ppb file extension,

- In Version 15.1 baselines are saved as part of the Live (current) project file which is in *.pp format. Thus a single *.pp file contains the current project data and all baselines making sharing a complete project simpler as you only have to share one file, but the file may become very large,

- Version 15.2 reintroduced to option of keeping baseline files separate as in earlier versions of Powerproject and this has not changed in Version 16,

- You may export the baseline to a separate *.pp file in order to supply a person with a copy of a Baseline or to make a *.pp file smaller, this is because Baseline file does not include formatting,

- You may import a baseline and specify how to map the imported tasks to the current project tasks,

- You may also import Primavera XER file as a baseline.

Page 277

277

EASTWOOD HARRIS PTY LTD.

Creating Baselines...

To create a Baseline:

- Select relevant tasks to set a partial baseline,

- Select **Project**, **Properties**, **Baseline Manager** to open the **Baseline/What If Manager** form,

- Click **New** to run the **Baseline Wizard**:

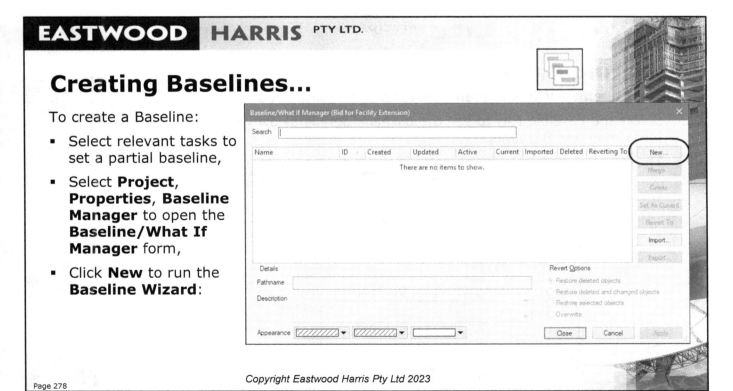

Page 278

278

EASTWOOD HARRIS PTY LTD.

Creating Baselines...

- Enter the baseline **Name** and **Description** in the **Details** form and select **Next**,
- **Embed the baseline in the file** decides if a separate Baseline file is created,
- The **Destination** form is only displayed when the Baseline is not embedded,
- Complete the **Scope** form and select **Next**,
- Check the details in **Summary** and select **Finish** to save the Baseline:

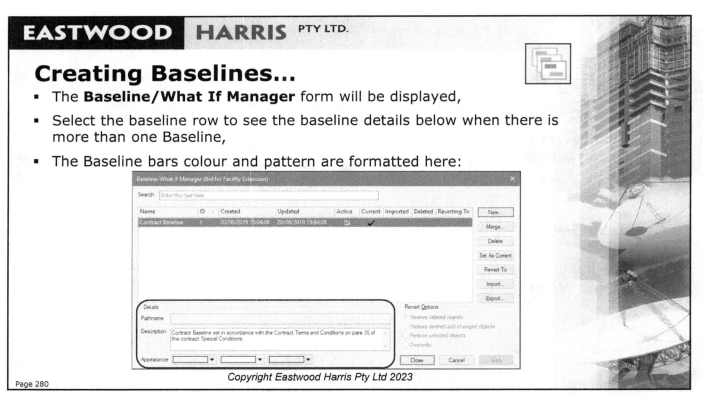

Page 279

Copyright Eastwood Harris Pty Ltd 2023

279

EASTWOOD HARRIS PTY LTD.

Creating Baselines...

- The **Baseline/What If Manager** form will be displayed,
- Select the baseline row to see the baseline details below when there is more than one Baseline,
- The Baseline bars colour and pattern are formatted here:

Page 280

Copyright Eastwood Harris Pty Ltd 2023

280

EASTWOOD HARRIS PTY LTD.

Creating Baselines

- This baseline has a tick under the **Current** heading,

- When there are multiple Baselines one only may be checked as **Current** which allows you to change the **Current Baseline** in the **Baseline/What if Manager** form,

- All reports that refer to the **Current Baseline** will be adjusted accordingly,

- This is a very useful feature when you wish to show the last period baseline in your reports and you just have to change the Current Baseline in one place and not have to change lots of Views.

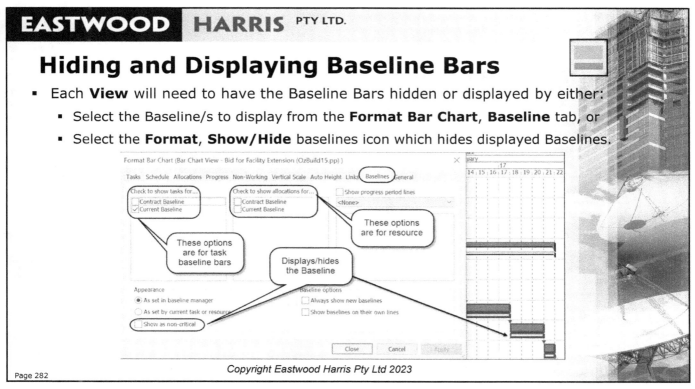

Page 281

281

EASTWOOD HARRIS PTY LTD.

Hiding and Displaying Baseline Bars

- Each **View** will need to have the Baseline Bars hidden or displayed by either:
    - Select the Baseline/s to display from the **Format Bar Chart**, **Baseline** tab, or
    - Select the **Format**, **Show/Hide** baselines icon which hides displayed Baselines.

Page 282

282

EASTWOOD HARRIS PTY LTD.

Changing the appearance of baseline tasks

- The Baseline is displayed as a second bar which is the lower bar in yellow in the picture,

- To format size of the bars and the distance between the tasks and the baseline,

  - Right click in the bar chart area,

  - Select **Format Bar Chart**,

  - Go to the **Vertical Scale** tab and at the bottom left adjust Task to baseline gap.

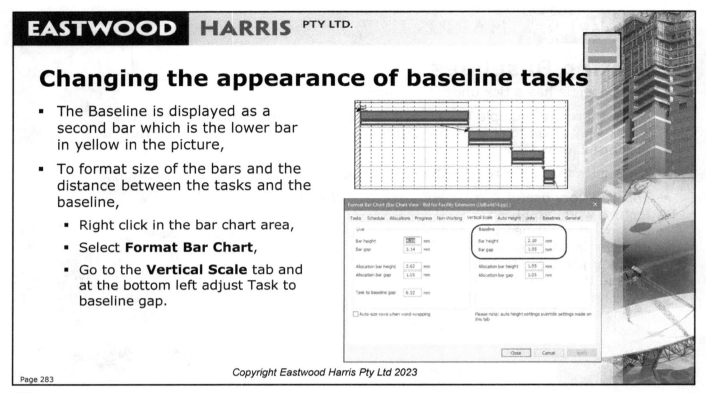

Page 283

Copyright Eastwood Harris Pty Ltd 2023

283

EASTWOOD HARRIS PTY LTD.

To change the colour of Baseline Bars

- Select the **Project**, **Properties**, **Baseline Manager**,
- Select the appropriate baseline,
- Select the **Appearance** and colour of the baseline bar in the bottom left of the form:

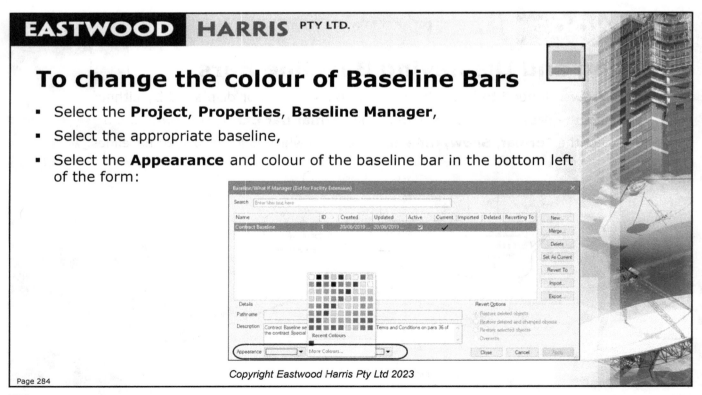

Page 284

Copyright Eastwood Harris Pty Ltd 2023

284

EASTWOOD HARRIS PTY LTD.

Revert and Merging a Baseline

- Use the **Revert** function to convert a Baseline file into the Live (Current) Project, click with care,

- **Merging** a Baseline brings in missing data from a Live Project into the Baseline, again use with care,

- Before using either the **Revert** and **Merging** functions take a copy of your programme.

Copyright Eastwood Harris Pty Ltd 2023

285

EASTWOOD HARRIS PTY LTD.

14 – BASELINES - SUMMARY

We have covered in this module:

- How to create a Baseline

- Display a Baseline bar in the Gantt Chart and

- Formatting a Baseline bar.

Copyright Eastwood Harris Pty Ltd 2023

286

EASTWOOD HARRIS PTY LTD.

Workshop 14 – Setting the Baseline

- The project has been approved and you will need to set a baseline.

Page 287

287

EASTWOOD HARRIS PTY LTD.

15 - UPDATING AN UNRESOURCED PROJECT

This module will cover the following topics:

- Concepts for Updating an Unresourced Project
- Multiple Reports Dates
- Displaying Progress
- Progress Options and Setting the Progress Date
- Understanding the Percent Complete fields
- Entering Progress
- Overall Percent Complete Weighting
- Task Work
- Rescheduling with Progress
- Workshop 15 - Updating the Schedule and Baseline Comparison.

Page 288

288

EASTWOOD HARRIS PTY LTD.

Updating an Unresourced Project

- The are many methods of updating progress and Powerproject has far more options than most competitors and some that are complex to understand,

- It is suggested that you decide what results you are seeking and then work out the options you require before you update your schedule,

- Document the **Options** and test them on a simple schedule,

- Then apply them to your working schedule,

- Organisations should create procedures and templates with all the **Schedule Options** set to simplify the setting up of project programmes for less experienced users,

- **Note:** It is generally accepted that a properly updated schedule will have all the completed work in the past with Actual Dates representing when the work was performed and all incomplete work in the future. This schedule would then provide a revised project finish date.

Copyright Eastwood Harris Pty Ltd 2023

289

EASTWOOD HARRIS PTY LTD.

Updating an Unresourced Project

There are two main methods used with Powerproject to update a schedule:

- The first method is to just enter the **Percent Complete** against each task which will show if activities are ahead or behind of the **Report Date**,

  - This does not reschedule incomplete work that is scheduled in the past forward in time into the future, or reschedule complete work scheduled in the future back to the past, both of these situations are illogical, and

  - This leaves a **Jagged Report Line**, and **NOT** considered a properly updated schedule,

- The second method is to **Straighten the Report Line** which reschedules:

  - Incomplete work into the future based on the logic and remaining durations, and

  - Moves complete work into the past, thus Actual Dates may not be correct but theses may be adjusted to produce a properly updated program,

- **Note:** P6 only updates a schedule with a **Straight Report Line** and this may be set as the default in Powerproject and the **Jagged Report Line** not used.

Copyright Eastwood Harris Pty Ltd 2023

290

EASTWOOD HARRIS PTY LTD.

Updating An Unresourced Project

- This module will look at two methods of updating a program with Powerproject,
- The main steps for monitoring progress are:
  - Set the **Reschedule Options** to reflect how you wish to update your schedule,
  - Saving a **Baseline** schedule, covered in the last module,
  - Record or mark-up progress as of a specific date, know in Powerproject as the **Report Date**,
  - Update the schedule,
  - Straightening the **Progress Line**, forcing all incomplete work into the future and complete work into the past,
  - Comparing and reporting actual progress against planned progress and revising the plan and schedule, as required.

Page 291

291

EASTWOOD HARRIS PTY LTD.

Understanding the Concepts

There are three stages in a task lifecycle:

- **Not Started** – The Early Start and Early Finish dates are calculated from the Predecessors, Constraints, and Task Duration,

- **In-Progress** – The task has an Actual Start date but is not complete:
  - The task is assigned an Actual Start date, normally entered in the past in relationship to the Report Date, which will override the Start Constraints and Start links that were originally used to calculate the Early Start,
  - The Finish Date will be calculated from the Report Date and the Remaining Duration,

- **Complete** – The task is in the past, the Actual Start and Actual Finish dates are manually entered in the past and they override all logic and constraints.

Page 292

292

EASTWOOD HARRIS PTY LTD.

Understanding Multiple Report Dates and Progress Periods

- Microsoft Project, P6 and many other scheduling software packages have one **Data Date** (P6 term) or **Status Date** (Microsoft Project term) that is moved forward in time each time a project schedule is updated,

- Powerproject allows the creation of multiple **Report Dates** and then you have a choice of either using:

  - One **Project Report Date** which may be displayed and moved forward in time as the project progresses. This is the process P6 and Microsoft Project use, or

  - Multiple **Project Report Dates** which creates **Progress Periods** between pairs of **Project Report Dates**. This will in turn enable the display the progress in each **Progress Period**.

Page 293

293

EASTWOOD HARRIS PTY LTD.

Creating Multiple Progress Periods

To create multiple **Report Dates** which in turn creates multiple **Progress Periods**:

- Open the **Library Explorer**,

- Select **Progress Period**,

- There will normally be at least one date and you may rename it, then

- Add additional **Report Dates** every week or month to reflect when you plan to update your schedule:

Name	Report date	Line style
Week 1	13/12/2021 00:00	
Week 2	20/12/2021 00:00	
Week 3	27/12/2021 00:00	
Week 4	3/01/2022 00:00	
Week 5	10/01/2022 00:00	
Week 6	17/01/2022 00:00	
Week 7	24/01/2022 00:00	
Week 8	31/01/2022 00:00	

Page 294

294

EASTWOOD HARRIS PTY LTD.

Setting the Progress Entry Period Date

- When multiple **Progress Periods** are created only one may be set as the **Progress Entry Period** for the update you are about to enter,

- The current **Progress Period** has a red tick against it in the **Project View** and may be set by either:

  - In the **Project View** right click and select **Progress Entry Period** or

  - In the **Reschedule Progress Period Warning** form,

- **Note:** There are two date fields in the **Reschedule Progress Period Warning** form and it is best to keep them the same by setting the **Straighten progress period** to **Progress entry period**.

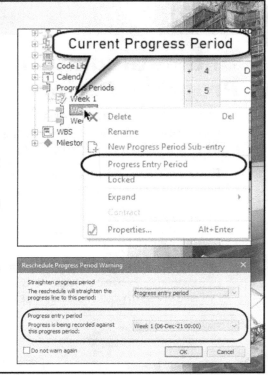

EASTWOOD HARRIS PTY LTD.

Displaying Progress Periods on the Gantt Chart

To view the progress lines:

- Open the **Format Bar Chart** form, **Progress** tab,

- Check the **Lines On** check box to display **Progress Lines**,

- Check the boxes for **Progress Lines** you wish to display,

- **Line style** allows a:

  - **Jagged Progress Line** or

  - **Straight Progress Line** or

  - **Straight Progress Line on Summaries/Hammocks** is used with the **Jagged Line** option but is Straight on Hammocks and Summaries,

  - The picture displays a **Jagged Progress Line**:

Displaying Progress Periods on the Gantt Chart

- If you check the **Progress entry line date only** option, Powerproject will only show the **Report Date** line of the selected **Progress Entry Period** selected in the Project View and not display any other Progress Lines:

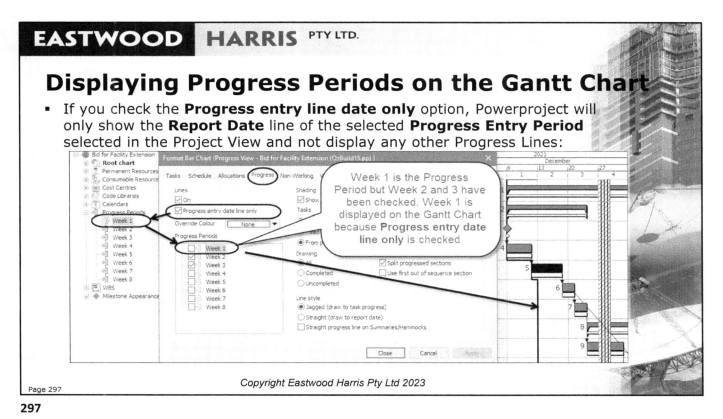

Copyright Eastwood Harris Pty Ltd 2023

Page 297

297

Displaying progress in the bar chart

Before we assign progress you need to ensure that progress will be displayed,

- **Show Shading** displays the progress shading,

- **Default shading** shades half of the bar and

- **Solid shading** shades the whole bar,

- **Fixed Shading** shades progress for each period in the colour selected and

- **From Period** shades the progress for each period in the same colour as the **Progress Period Line** for the period progress was recorded.

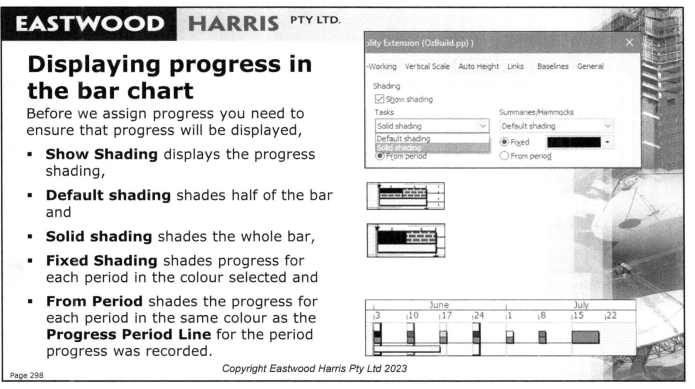

Copyright Eastwood Harris Pty Ltd 2023

Page 298

298

EASTWOOD HARRIS PTY LTD.

Progress Options...

- Before entering progress you must check your **Progress Options**,

- Select **File**, **Options**,

- Select the **Progress** tab,

- **Snapping** is very useful as you are able to keep the **Duration Remaining** to round days and in turn one day tasks do not start in the middle of the day and span two days,

- The defaults are usually good and should not be changed unless they are well understood,

- See the **Powerproject Help** for details.

Options for Bid for Facility Extension

Edit | Assign | View | Format | Progress | Reschedule | File Locations | Calendars | Spreadsheet | General

Progress entry mode
- ● Update duration in step
- ○ Fill to progress line
  - ☐ Do not recompute remaining after overall percent update

Snapping
- ☑ Snap actual/remaining duration to snapping unit
- Progress snapping unit: Days

Jagged Progress View
- ● Use current baseline
- ○ Use project baseline(s)

Ribbon, toolbar progress controls and percent complete field
- ● Duration percent complete
- ○ Overall percent complete

Miscellaneous
- ☐ Enter progress shows 'User Percent Complete'
- ☐ In Progress from allocations, recalculate durations where allocation is calculated
- ☐ Update progress via duration remaining
- Progress method: Duration - Approximate
- Site Progress Login: Company ID and Username

[Close]

Copyright Eastwood Harris Pty Ltd 2023

299

EASTWOOD HARRIS PTY LTD.

Progress Options...

- Under **Progress Entry Mode** decide if you would like to:

  - **Update duration in step**, or

  - **Fill to progress line**, this is similar to the way P6 calculates:

  - **Fill to progress line** with **Do not recomputed remaining after overall percent complete**:

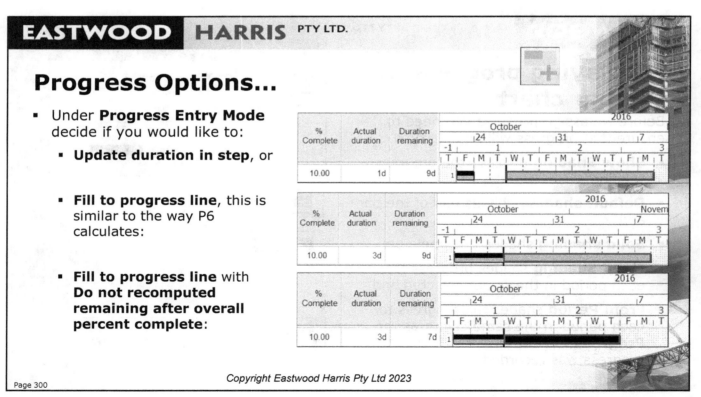

Copyright Eastwood Harris Pty Ltd 2023

300

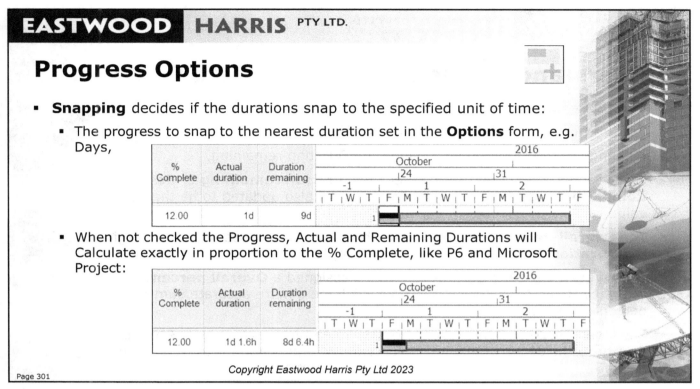

Progress Options

- **Snapping** decides if the durations snap to the specified unit of time:
  - The progress to snap to the nearest duration set in the **Options** form, e.g. Days,

  - When not checked the Progress, Actual and Remaining Durations will Calculate exactly in proportion to the % Complete, like P6 and Microsoft Project:

301

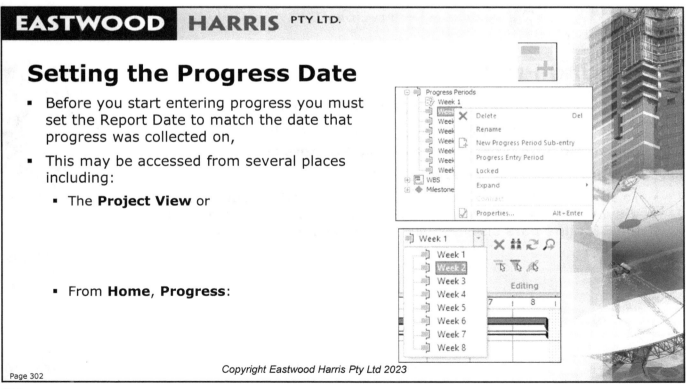

Setting the Progress Date

- Before you start entering progress you must set the Report Date to match the date that progress was collected on,
- This may be accessed from several places including:
  - The **Project View** or

  - From **Home**, **Progress**:

302

EASTWOOD HARRIS PTY LTD.

Understanding the Percent Complete fields

- Duration = Actual duration + Duration remaining,
- Percent Complete = Actual duration/Duration,
- A change to the Duration will change the Duration remaining,
- When a task is updated using either the **Duration remaining** or **Percent Complete** the **Overall Percent Complete** is also updated to be the same value,
- The **Overall Percent Complete** may be edited afterwards without changing the **Duration remaining** or **Percent Complete**,
- The **Overall Percent Complete** may be assigned a **Overall percent weighting** and then Summary Tasks will have a more accurate summary percent complete,
- The **User Percent Complete** is like the P6 and Microsoft Project **Physical % Complete** fields may have any value entered and is not linked to any other fields.

Page 303   *Copyright Eastwood Harris Pty Ltd 2023*

303

EASTWOOD HARRIS PTY LTD.

Entering Progress...

- There are several ways to enter progress, including:
  - **Bar and Task Properties** form, **Task**, **Progress** tab,
  - **Bar and Task Properties** view, **Task**, **Progress** tab,
  - Using a **Table** with the appropriate columns,
- To show the progress specific columns you should consider creating a **View** with an associated **Table** that displays the progress columns, has the **Baseline bars** displayed and **Progress Lines** formatted as required.

Copyright Eastwood Harris Pty Ltd 2023

Page 304

304

EASTWOOD HARRIS PTY LTD.

Entering Progress

- A progress Table would have the following columns:
  - Line Number and Name
  - Actual Start and Actual Finish
  - Duration, Actual Duration and Duration Remaining
  - Percent Complete
  - Planned Percent Complete (Pointed to the current baseline)
  - Finish variance (Pointed to the current baseline)
- Any progress entered into the Percent Complete column or a Duration column will be displayed on the task bar:

Line	Name	Start	Actual start	Finish	Actual finish	Duration	Actual duration	Duration remaining	User percent complete	Percent complete	Planned % Complete	Finish variance	September 24 1	1 2	8 3	October 15 4 2018
1	Task	25-Sep-18	25-Sep-18	16-Oct-18		16d	6d	10d	200.00	37.50	50%	-2d				

EASTWOOD HARRIS PTY LTD.

Overall Percent Complete Weighting...

- One issue with Microsoft Project is that **Summary Task Percent Completes** are calculated from the sum of the **Non Summary Task Actual Durations** divided by the sum of the **Non Summary Task Durations** which in turn leads to misleading Summary task **Actual Durations**, **Remaining Durations** and **% Complete**,
- Also P6 will not give a **Summary % Complete** against **WBS Nodes** when **Physical % Complete** is used,
- The Powerproject **Overall Percent complete** allows a weighting to be assigned to the tasks enabling an accurate user defined **Summary Task % Complete**,
- When tasks are created they are all equally weighted, so when each task is completed an equal amount is shown to have been progressed.

Overall Percent Complete Weighting

- The first picture shows a summary task with all the Overall percent complete weighting of the sub tasks are the same,

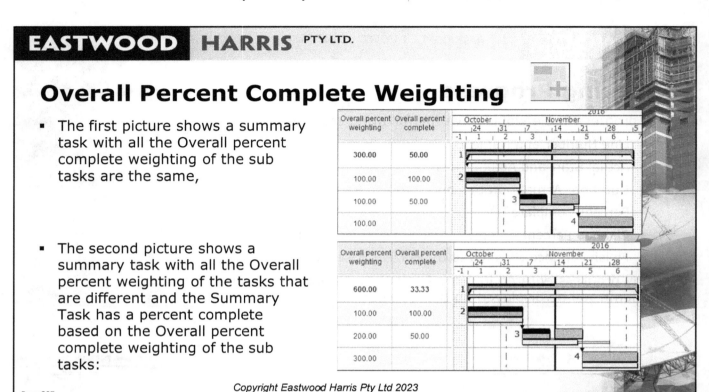

- The second picture shows a summary task with all the Overall percent weighting of the tasks that are different and the Summary Task has a percent complete based on the Overall percent complete weighting of the sub tasks:

307

Task Work

- The **Task Work** fields allow a task duration to be driven by a **Task Work** and a **Task Work Rate** without resources allocated to tasks,
- The information may be entered in columns or the **Bar and Task Properties** form,
- In Version 15 this may now be displayed in a graph:

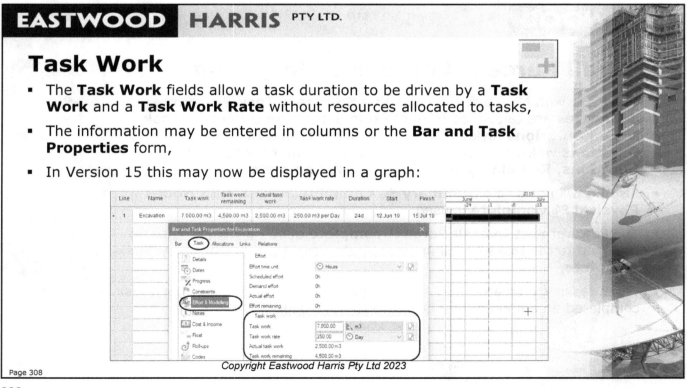

308

EASTWOOD HARRIS PTY LTD.

Task Work Modelling

- The **Options**, **Edit** tab determines whether the **Work Rate** or **Work** is changed when the task duration is changed:

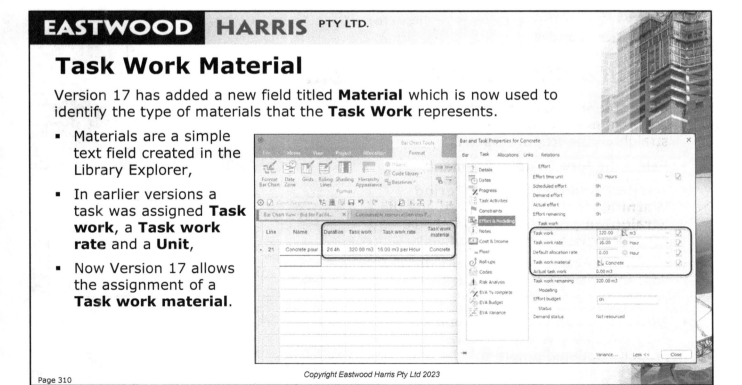

(Options for Task Work dialog — Edit tab)

```
Options for Task Work                                                    ×

( Edit )  Assign  View  Format  Progress  Reschedule  File Locations  Calendars  Spreadsheet  General

   Tasks
   When editing start or finish in spreadsheet    ○ Change duration        ● Move task
   When inserting by spreadsheet                  ● Create subheading      ○ Create task
   When creating tasks                            ○ Copy bar name          ● Leave name empty
   ☑ Inherit attributes from neighbouring task    ☑ Charts inherit display attributes from parent

   Task work
   Editing duration for task-work driven task updates   ○ Work       ● Work rate
   Task work rate determiner                            [ per ]

   Costs
```

- This is similar to the P6 resource options of:

  - Fixed Duration and Units = Work

  - Fixed Duration and Units/Time = Work Rate.

309

EASTWOOD HARRIS PTY LTD.

Task Work Material

Version 17 has added a new field titled **Material** which is now used to identify the type of materials that the **Task Work** represents.

- Materials are a simple text field created in the Library Explorer,

- In earlier versions a task was assigned **Task work**, a **Task work rate** and a **Unit**,

- Now Version 17 allows the assignment of a **Task work material**.

310

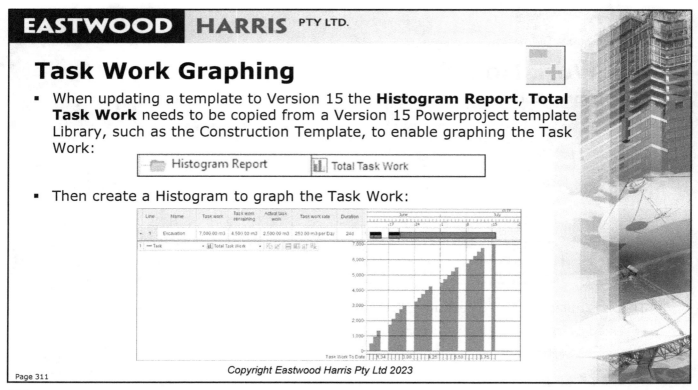

EASTWOOD HARRIS PTY LTD.

Task Work Graphing

- When updating a template to Version 15 the **Histogram Report**, **Total Task Work** needs to be copied from a Version 15 Powerproject template Library, such as the Construction Template, to enable graphing the Task Work:

Histogram Report	Total Task Work

- Then create a Histogram to graph the Task Work:

Copyright Eastwood Harris Pty Ltd 2023

Page 311

311

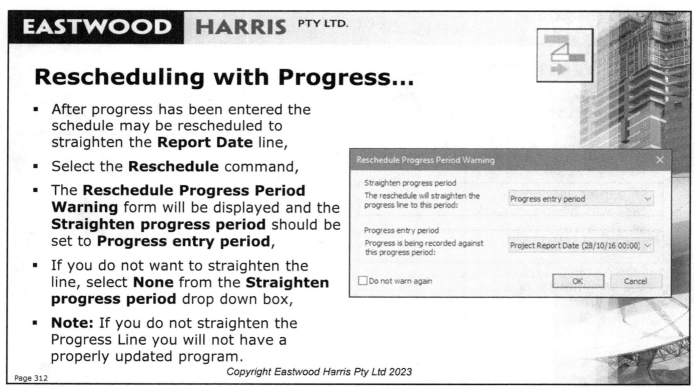

EASTWOOD HARRIS PTY LTD.

Rescheduling with Progress...

- After progress has been entered the schedule may be rescheduled to straighten the **Report Date** line,

- Select the **Reschedule** command,

- The **Reschedule Progress Period Warning** form will be displayed and the **Straighten progress period** should be set to **Progress entry period**,

- If you do not want to straighten the line, select **None** from the **Straighten progress period** drop down box,

- **Note:** If you do not straighten the Progress Line you will not have a properly updated program.

Copyright Eastwood Harris Pty Ltd 2023

Page 312

312

EASTWOOD HARRIS PTY LTD.

Rescheduling with Progress

- Scheduling will straighten **Progress Line** and:
  - Push incomplete portions of tasks into the future and
  - Push completed work into the past:
- **Before** scheduling

- **After** scheduling
- **Note:** Actual Dates will change when a complete part of a task was in the future,
- At this point it would be prudent to ensure the actual dates match when work actually started and finished, especially if your are entering into litigation.

Page 313

313

EASTWOOD HARRIS PTY LTD.

Jagged Line to Straight Line Display

- If you have followed the update progress over multiple periods and Straightened the Progress Line each time, then you will have a project which will show:
  - The progress for each period, and
  - A revised end date of the project:

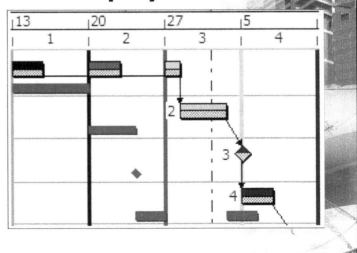

Page 314

314

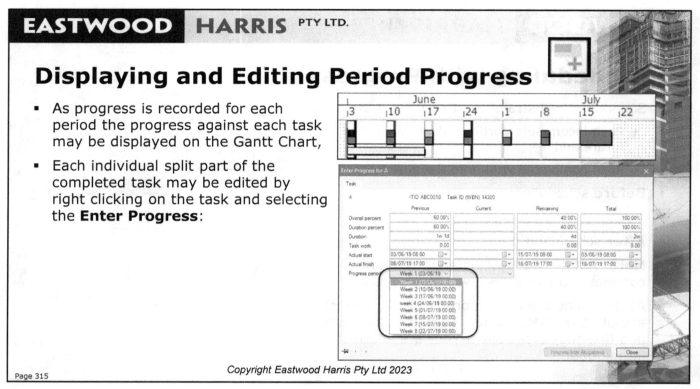

EASTWOOD HARRIS PTY LTD.

Displaying and Editing Period Progress

- As progress is recorded for each period the progress against each task may be displayed on the Gantt Chart,

- Each individual split part of the completed task may be edited by right clicking on the task and selecting the **Enter Progress**:

Page 315

315

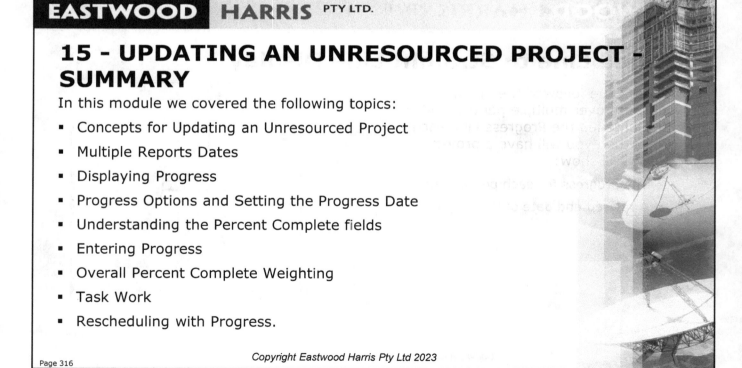

EASTWOOD HARRIS PTY LTD.

15 - UPDATING AN UNRESOURCED PROJECT - SUMMARY

In this module we covered the following topics:

- Concepts for Updating an Unresourced Project
- Multiple Reports Dates
- Displaying Progress
- Progress Options and Setting the Progress Date
- Understanding the Percent Complete fields
- Entering Progress
- Overall Percent Complete Weighting
- Task Work
- Rescheduling with Progress.

Page 316

316

EASTWOOD HARRIS PTY LTD.

Workshop 15 - Updating the Schedule and Baseline Comparison

- At the end of the first week you have to update the schedule and report progress and slippage.

317

EASTWOOD HARRIS PTY LTD.

16 - LIBRARY EXPLORER

- Project files contain many objects such as resources, codes, calendars, and currency units,

- These are stored in the Library Explorer,

- Objects may be simply copied from the Library Explorer in one project to a Library Explorer in another project.

318

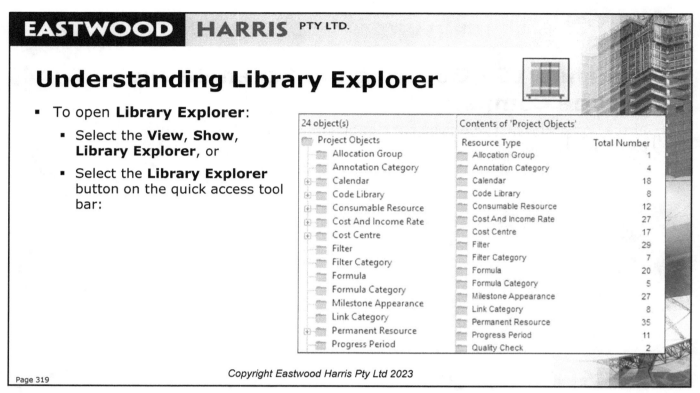

Understanding Library Explorer

- To open **Library Explorer**:
  - Select the **View**, **Show**, **Library Explorer**, or
  - Select the **Library Explorer** button on the quick access tool bar:

Page 319

Copyright Eastwood Harris Pty Ltd 2023

319

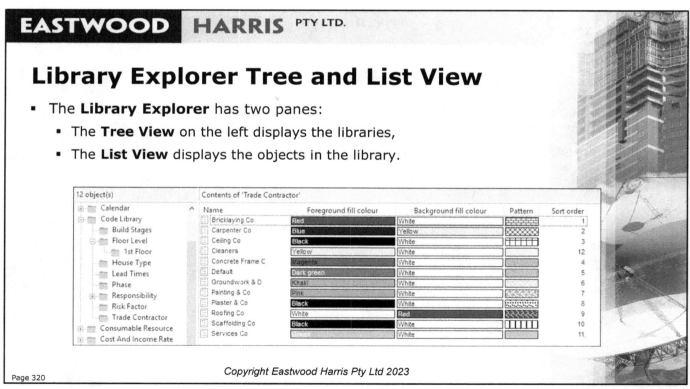

Library Explorer Tree and List View

- The **Library Explorer** has two panes:
  - The **Tree View** on the left displays the libraries,
  - The **List View** displays the objects in the library.

Page 320

Copyright Eastwood Harris Pty Ltd 2023

320

Customising Library Explorer...

- All libraries are not displayed by default,
- To show or hide libraries right click a blank area of the **List View** then select **Show Libraries**:

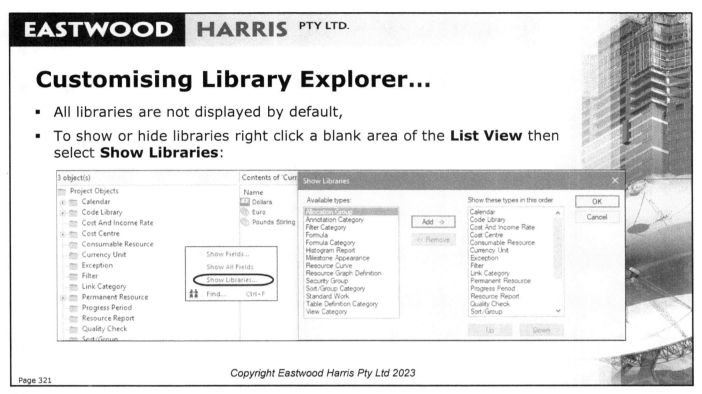

Page 321

321

Customising Library Explorer

- Select libraries in the **Library Explorer** from the right-hand list select **Remove** to remove a library,
- Select libraries in the **Library Explorer** from the right-hand list select **Add** to add a library,
- Use the **Up** and **Down** buttons to reorder the Libraries, an alphabetical order is useful:

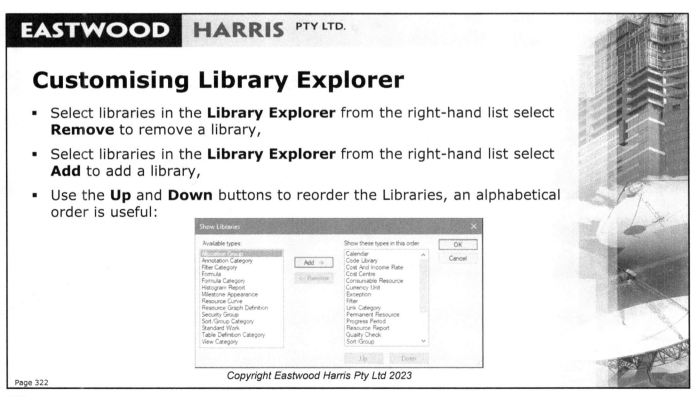

Page 322

322

EASTWOOD HARRIS PTY LTD.

Workshop 16 – Library Explorer

- We will reformat the Library Explorer in this workshop.

Page 323

323

EASTWOOD HARRIS PTY LTD.

17 - USER DEFINABLE FIELDS & WBS

- Powerproject allows the creation of **User Defined Fields** with formulae,
- For example, you may want to add a specific comment field,
- These have a similar functionality to Microsoft Project Custom Fields in terms of the ability to assign formulae to calculate new data from other fields,
- Also, they are similar to P6 User Definable fields but a lot more powerful.

Page 324

324

EASTWOOD HARRIS PTY LTD.

Creating User Fields for your projects

- User **Field Manager** will not operate until the project has been saved,

- Select **Project**, **Properties**, **User Field Manager** command,

- Select **Add** to create a field,

- Select the type of field that you want to create and

- Assign a name for the field, it must not have spaces.

Page 325

Copyright Eastwood Harris Pty Ltd 2023

325

EASTWOOD HARRIS PTY LTD.

Work Breakdown Structure

- Work Breakdown Structure (WBS), a hierarchical structure which usually identifies the major deliverables,

- Like P6, the WBS may be created before activities are added and allows another method of organizing the activities,

- A well-structured WBS should:

  - Include all the project deliverables and

  - Be set at the appropriate level for summarizing project activities and reporting project progress,

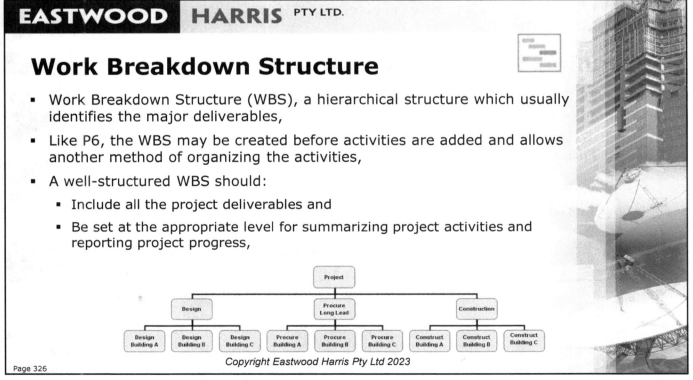

Page 326

Copyright Eastwood Harris Pty Ltd 2023

326

EASTWOOD HARRIS PTY LTD.

Creating a WBS Structure

- Select Project, Properties, Work Breakdown Structure command,
- Create the WBS Codes and
- Click Close:

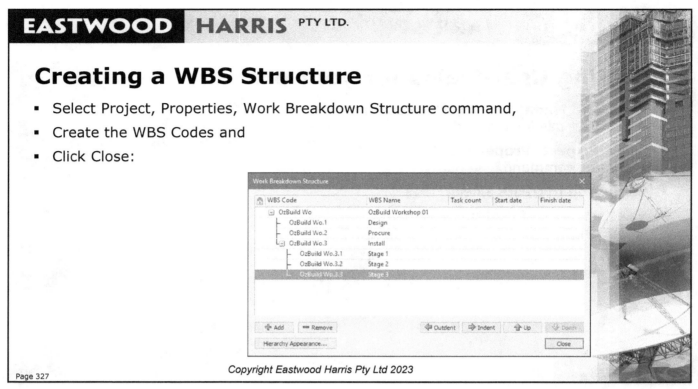

Copyright Eastwood Harris Pty Ltd 2023

Page 327

327

EASTWOOD HARRIS PTY LTD.

Assigning WBS Codes to Tasks

- The WBS Codes are assigned to tasks form **Project View** the in the same way as calendars and Codes,
- **Note:** To change the display of the WBS Hierarchy from **Code** to **Name**, select **File**, **Options**, **Views**,

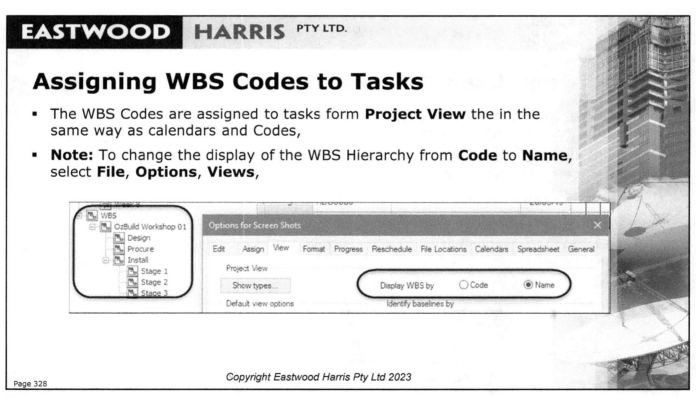

Copyright Eastwood Harris Pty Ltd 2023

Page 328

328

EASTWOOD HARRIS PTY LTD.

WBS Codes and Columns

- WBS Codes may be viewed and edited in the following columns
  - **WBS Code Identification,**
  - **WBS Name Identification:**

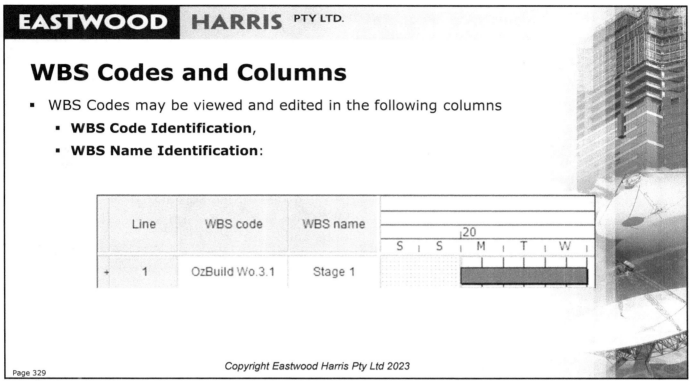

Page 329

329

EASTWOOD HARRIS PTY LTD.

To Display by WBS

- To see the task grouped by WBS, you will need to:
- Set the **Hierarchy Appearance** from the **Work Breakdown** form, and
- Create or apply **a Sort and Group** by WBS:

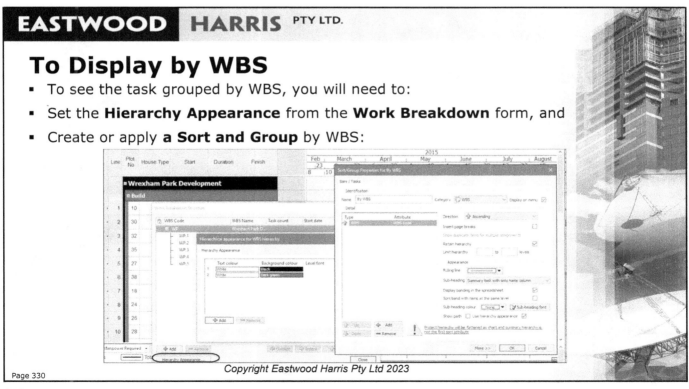

Page 330

330

EASTWOOD HARRIS PTY LTD.

Course Close

We have covered the following topics:

- Introduction to Powerproject and Creating a project
- Navigation and Setting Options
- Calendars
- Tasks and Milestones
- Summary Tasks
- Linking Tasks to create a Critical Path Schedule
- Constraints

- Other Task Types
- Formatting the Display
- Code Libraries
- Filters
- Organising Tasks using Sort and Groups
- Printing and Reports
- Baselines
- Updating an Unresourced Project
- Library Explorer
- User Definable Fields and WBS.

Page 331

Copyright Eastwood Harris Pty Ltd 2023

331

EASTWOOD HARRIS PTY LTD.

Review Expectations

- Any questions,
- Complete Feedback Sheet,
- Have we met your expectations?

Page 332

Copyright Eastwood Harris Pty Ltd 2023

332

www.ingramcontent.com/pod-product-compliance
Lightning Source LLC
Chambersburg PA
CBHW061631080326
40690CB00058B/4366